Threading the Sovereign's Needle

International Investment Law and Arbitration

Volumes published in this Brill Research Perspectives title are listed at *brill.com/rpia*

Threading the Sovereign's Needle

A Philosophical Deconstruction of an Investor-State Tribunal's Authority to Award Interim Relief in Relation to Criminal Proceedings

By

Alexander G. Leventhal

BRILL

LEIDEN | BOSTON

This paperback book edition is simultaneously published as issue 3.4 of *International Investment Law and Arbitration*, DOI:10.1163/24055778-12340010.

Library Congress Control Number: 2021939435

Typeface for the Latin, Greek, and Cyrillic scripts: “Brill”. See and download: brill.com/brill-typeface.

ISBN 978-90-04-46930-3 (paperback)
ISBN 978-90-04-46931-0 (e-book)

This book is printed on acid-free paper and produced in a sustainable manner.

Contents

Threading the Sovereign's Needle

A Philosophical Deconstruction of an Investor-State Tribunal's Authority to Award Interim Relief in Relation to Criminal Proceedings

Alexander G. Leventhal
Of Counsel, Quinn Emanuel Urquhart & Sullivan LLP
alexanderleventhal@quinnemanuel.com

Abstract

An investor-State tribunal enjoys significant authority once a dispute is referred to it. Among a tribunal's unquestioned powers is the power to order interim relief—including with respect to the most sovereign of a State's conduct: its enforcement of its criminal law. In exercising these powers, an investor-State tribunal goes beyond the role traditionally assigned to it—i.e. to award damages for prejudice caused by a treaty breach—and dictates sovereign conduct. While the applicable treaty, arbitral rules, or law of the seat may not offer specific instructions, arbitral tribunals deciding on such interim relief requests can rely on a significant body of case law. That case law reflects a coherent approach to a thorny question, even though outcomes may vary. This article will deconstruct that coherent approach—from the foundations of the tribunal's authority to order interim relief in respect to pendant criminal proceedings, to the rights that such relief may protect, to the requirements for ordering such relief, as well the effect of such relief and its duration in addition to any recourse for non-compliance.

Keywords

Investor-State – arbitration – criminal proceedings – sovereign – philosophy – treaty arbitration

 | DOI:10.1163/9789004469310_002

Introduction[1]

As ancient as the law itself, the power to grant interim relief is etched in the basic framework of all legal systems the world over.[2] In both civil[3] and common law[4] jurisdictions, for example, adjudicators may issue interim orders preventing third parties from assisting a litigant to siphon assets out of the adjudicator's jurisdiction pending final adjudication of the merits.[5] Adjudicators may also order a litigant to take, or refrain from taking, specific actions on an interim basis—for example, by way of an anti-suit injunction ordering a party to withdraw or refrain from initiating parallel litigation.[6] This power, which, in the words of UK Supreme Court Justice Lord Collins, is "an integral part of the process of the peaceful settlement of disputes,"[7] lies at the heart of any adjudicator's own ability to render a final and enforceable decision on the merits.

International law is no stranger to interim relief. Not only does the International Court of Justice regularly "indicate" interim relief pursuant to Article 41 of its Statute, investor-State tribunals also routinely "recommend" or "order" such relief—many on the basis of Article 47 of the ICSID Convention, which itself is based on Article 41 of the ICJ's Statute.

However, while an investor-State tribunal's power to order interim relief may be sown from the same cloth as that of permanent international law bodies (like the ICJ), both forms of relief stand worlds apart. Unlike those permanent bodies, investor-State tribunals are generally called upon to order interim relief that is incidental to the relief on the merits because any economic damage can be compensated with a financial award. Moreover,

1 Alexander G. Leventhal is Of Counsel in the international arbitration department of Quinn Emanuel Urquhart & Sullivan LLP ("Quinn Emanuel"). The opinions expressed in this work are his alone and not the opinions of Quinn Emanuel.

2 *See* C. Miles, Provisional Measures before International Courts and Tribunals (Cambridge University Press, 2017), Chapter 2: Origins of Provisional Matters.

3 *See e.g.* French Code of Civil Procedure, Article 484.

4 *See e.g.* 18 CFR § 385.1113.

5 *See e.g. Mareva Compania Naviera SA v. International Bulkcarriers SA*, [1975] 2 Lloyd's Rep 509 (C.A. 23 June 1975), [1980] 1 All ER 21.

6 *See e.g. Microsoft Corp. v. Motorola, Inc.*, 696 F.3d 872, 886 (9th Cir. 2012); *Allendale Mut. Ins. Co. v. Bull Data Sys., Inc.*, 10 F.3d 425, 431 (7th Cir. 1993); *Seattle Totems Hockey Club v. Nat'l Hockey League*, 652 F.2d 852, 855–56 (9th Cir. 1981); *Lenovo (United States) Inc. and others v. IPCom GmbH & Co. Kg*, French Court of Appeal, No. 14/2020 (Mar. 3, 2015).

7 L. Collins, "Provisional and Protective Measures in International Litigation," in Recueil Des Cours, Collected Courses of The Hague Academy of International Law, Vol. 234 (1992), p. 215.

where an investor-State tribunal *does* grant interim relief, it enjoins conduct that is of an eminently sovereign nature *in favour of a private party*.

A recent survey confirms that over 20% of requests for interim measures of publicly available decisions sought a stay of the most primordial sovereign police power, a State's right to pursue a criminal investigation or criminal prosecution.[8] This is significant. When an investor-State tribunal orders such relief, it dons sovereign regalia and—for the purposes of the interim application—plays the role of the prince, one that, in the works of Shakespeare and other authors, may be valiant or timorous, but always a character with boundless authority.

Faced with this high task, will the tribunal act with the conviction of Henry V, charging once more into the breach, or with the equivocation of Hamlet, questioning the consequences of its own existence, to be or not to be? On first impression, the record would appear to be mixed (at best) or incongruous (at worst)—some tribunals, like the *Hydro* tribunal, have ordered the full and unequivocal suspension of a high-profile prosecution[9] while others, like the *Teinver* tribunal, declined to order cessation even of the allegedly trumped-up criminal prosecution of counsel.[10]

Yet, first impressions may be deceiving, and a closer look of the decisions signed by some of the most eminent names in international law reveals a coherent line of thought from the very first decisions of the Permanent Court of International Justice to the most recent investor-State tribunal decisions.

This article will draw from those decisions the fundaments of an interim relief philosophy in relation to this most sovereign conduct. It will do so in five acts. First, this article will address the foundations of an investor-State tribunal's authority to order interim relief in relation to criminal law matters (I). Second, it will examine the types of rights whose protection merits an order for interim relief (II). Third, it will explore how investor-State tribunals have addressed the requirements to issue such relief (III). Fourth, it will look at whether such an order is binding on the parties and for how long (IV). And finally, this article examine what tools exist to enforce the interim relief in the event of non-compliance (V).

---

8 2019 EMPIRICAL STUDY: PROVISIONAL MEASURES IN INVESTOR-STATE ARBITRATION [available at https://www.biicl.org/publications/2019-empirical-study-provisional-measures-in-investorstate-arbitration] (last visited on Apr. 7, 2021).

9 *Hydro S.r.l. and others v. Republic of Albania*, ICSID Case No. ARB/15/28, Order on Provisional Measures (Mar. 3, 2016).

10 *Teinver S.A., Transportes de Cercanías S.A. and Autobuses Urbanos del Sur S.A. v. Argentine Republic*, ICSID Case No. ARB/09/1, Decision on Provisional Measures (Apr. 8, 2016).

1 Foundations

King Edward IV
Her looks do argue her replete with modesty;
Her words do show her wit incomparable;
All her perfections challenge sovereignty:
One way or other, she is for a king;
And she shall be my love, or else my queen.—
Say that King Edward take thee for his queen?

Queen Elizabeth
Tis better said than done, my gracious lord:
I am a subject fit to jest withal,
But far unfit to be a sovereign.

W. Shakespeare, Henry VI, Part III, *lns. 1569–1575*

How does a private arbitral tribunal "unfit to be a sovereign" step into sovereign shoes? Any analysis of an investor-State tribunal's authority to grant interim relief begins where it ends: State sovereignty.

Sovereignty refers to the idea that a State has the exclusive right to exercise criminal law authority within its territory. A State's police power to investigate and prosecute violations of its criminal law is, in the words of the tribunal in *Caratube v. Kazakhstan* (Professor Dr. Karl-Heinz Böckstiegel (chair), Dr. Kamal Hossain, Dr. Gavan Griffith QC), the "most obvious and undisputed part of the sovereign right of a state to implement and enforce its national law on its territory."[11] So central is this function to a State's sovereign role that a foreign jurisdiction, without a treaty or other agreement, will not assist or enforce the acts of foreign criminal law authorities within its own territory.[12]

However, sovereignty also refers to a State's ability to submit to the jurisdiction of an international law tribunal, like an investor-State tribunal, and to allow that body to order the restraint of its police powers. As the *Hydro* tribunal, comprised of Dr. Michael Pryles (chair), Ian Glick QC, and Charles Poncet, explained, a respondent State, "by signing the ICSID Convention, has accepted

---

11 *Caratube International Oil Company LLP v. Republic of Kazakhstan*, ICSID Case No. ARB/08/12, Decision Regarding Claimant's Application for Provisional Measures (July 31, 2009), para. 135.

12 R. Michaels, "Recognition and Enforcement of Foreign Judgments," Max Planck Encyclopedia of Public International Law (2009).

a tribunal's interference with its sovereign rights."[13] In so doing, a State, in effect, agrees to cede absolute authority over certain aspects of its sovereign prerogatives to an investor-State tribunal and is bound by the decision of that tribunal.[14]

Below, we look at the international law origins of interim relief in investor-State arbitration (**a**) as well as the tribunal's examination of its jurisdiction and admissibility (**b**) and the merits (**c**).

a *International Law Origins*

While investor-State arbitration has only existed for a half-century, its roots stretch deep into a rich history of international law dispute resolution.

The power to render "interlocutory or preparatory judgments" has been among a tribunal's powers from the very first codification of arbitral procedure by the *Institut de droit international* in 1873.[15] By the dawn of the 20th Century, that power had been exercised by at least one inter-State tribunal formed to resolve a dispute between Latin American countries and was enshrined in European treaties as well.[16]

Against this backdrop, Article 41 of the Statute of the Permanent Court of International Justice was drafted. That provision expressly granted that body "the power to indicate, if it considers the circumstances so require, any provisional measures which ought to be taken to reserve the respective rights of either party."[17] The PCIJ would go on to issue at least six decisions pursuant to this provision, including the decision in *Electricity Company of Sofia and*

13 *Hydro S.r.l. and others v. Republic of Albania*, ICSID Case No. ARB/15/28, Order on Provisional Measures (Mar. 3, 2016), para. 3.40. While the reference here is to the ICSID Convention, there is no reason to believe that the conclusion should be different for a non-ICSID tribunal as the *Hydro* tribunal's reference here is to the provision on interim measures.

14 United Nations, VIENNA CONVENTION ON THE LAW OF TREATIES, United Nations, Treaty Series, vol. 1155(May 23, 1969), p. 331 (stating in Article 26 that "[e]very treaty in force is binding upon the parties to it and must be performed by them in good faith").

15 C. Miles, PROVISIONAL MEASURES BEFORE INTERNATIONAL COURTS AND TRIBUNALS (Cambridge University Press, 2017), Chapter 3: Development by Early International Courts and Tribunals.

16 C. Miles, PROVISIONAL MEASURES BEFORE INTERNATIONAL COURTS AND TRIBUNALS (Cambridge University Press, 2017), Chapter 3: Development by Early International Courts and Tribunals.

17 League of Nations, STATUTE OF THE PERMANENT COURT OF INTERNATIONAL JUSTICE (Dec. 16, 1920).

Bulgaria, a decision which continues to be relied upon by the ICJ and even several investor-State tribunals.

Article 41 of the ICJ Statute—which is nearly identical to the same provision of the statute of its predecessor, the PCIJ—reads in relevant part as follows:

> The Court shall have the power to indicate, if it considers that circumstances so require, any provisional measures which ought to be taken to preserve the respective rights of either party.[18]

This provision has been applied in numerous State-to-State disputes *inter alia* to seek to prevent a State from executing foreign nationals convicted without notifying their Governments in alleged violation of relevant treaties,[19] to order States not to dispatch civilian, police, or security personnel into a disputed area,[20] to prevent one State from collecting evidence illegitimately for use against another State or interfering in the privileged communications of the latter State,[21] and to ensure that the civilians of one State are granted rights in another State.[22]

Beyond this provision, the ICJ has also evoked its "inherent powers of jurisdiction" when rendering interim relief.[23] As the Court explained in the *Nuclear Tests* case, such powers flow from the reality that, if the Court did not possess such powers, there would be a real risk that "the rights of the parties would get so prejudiced that the judgment of the Court when it came could be rendered meaningless."[24]

---

18 United Nations, STATUTE OF THE INTERNATIONAL COURT OF JUSTICE (Apr. 18, 1946).

19 *LaGrand (Germany v United States)*, [1999] ICJ Rep. 9 (Mar. 3, 1999); *Avena and Other Mexican Nationals (Mexico v United States)*, [2003] ICJ Rep. 77 (Feb. 5, 2003); *Jadhav Case (India v. Pakistan)* [2017] ICJ Rep. 231 (May 18, 2017).

20 *Certain Activities carried out by Nicaragua in the Border Area; Construction of a Road in Costa Rica along the San Juan River (Costa Rica v Nicaragua)*, [2013] ICJ Rep 354.

21 *Questions relating to the Seizure and Detention of Certain Documents and Data (Timor-Leste v Australia)*, [2014] ICGJ 472.

22 *Application of the International Convention on the Elimination of All Forms of Racial Discrimination (Qatar v. United Arab Emirates)* [2018] ICJ Rep. 406 (Jul. 23, 2018).

23 *Northern Cameroons, (Cameroon v United Kingdom)*, Separate Opinion of Judge Gerald Fitzmaurice, [1963] ICJ Rep. 15, 107. See also *Nuclear Tests (Australia v. France)*, [1973] ICJ Rep. 97 (June 22, 1973), 109; *Nuclear Tests (New Zealand v. France)*, [1973] ICJ Rep. 135, 145.

24 *Nuclear Tests (Australia v. France)*, Preliminary Objections, Order, [1973] ICJ Rep. 97 (June 22, 1973), 109; *Nuclear Tests (New Zealand v. France)*, [1973] ICJ Rep. 135 (June 22, 1975), 145.

While the ICSID Convention marks a pointed departure from prior practice in international law dispute resolution by adopting the dispute resolution model of international commercial arbitration, rather than creating a permanent body like the ICJ, it preserves the international law approach to interim relief. Article 47 of the ICSID Convention, which is based on Article 41 of the ICJ Statute, reads:

> Except as the parties otherwise agree, the Tribunal may, if it considers that the circumstances so require, recommend any provisional measures which should be taken to preserve the respective rights of either party.[25]

ICSID tribunals have drawn on the rich history of interim relief in international law when fashioning their own relief. Non-ICSID tribunals have mirrored the approach of ICSID tribunals (whose decisions are more widely published).

There is little doubt that these provisions (and inherent jurisdiction) empower a tribunal to order an interim measure in relation to criminal proceedings. While the *SGS* tribunal (which was seised with a request unrelated to criminal proceedings) offered in *dicta* that an investor-State tribunal "cannot enjoin a State conducting the normal processes of criminal, administrative and civil justice within its territory,"[26] other tribunals have expressly rejected that approach.[27] The *Caratube* tribunal (comprised of Karl-Heinz Böckstiegel (chair), Gavan Griffith QC, and Dr. Kamal Hossein) offered a pointed rebuke:

---

25 CONVENTION ON THE SETTLEMENT OF INVESTMENT DISPUTES BETWEEN STATES AND NATIONALS OF OTHER STATES (INTERNATIONAL CENTRE FOR SETTLEMENT OF INVESTMENT DISPUTES [ICSID]) 575 UNTS 159 (1966). While Article 47 uses the word "recommend," as explained below, there is no doubt that an ICSID tribunal's "recommendations" pursuant to Article 47 are binding. We therefore use "recommend" and "order" interchangeably in this article.

26 *SGS Société Générale de Surveilance v. Pakistan*, ICSID Case No. ARB/01/13, Procedural Order No. 2 (Oct. 16, 2002), p. 301. See also *Abaclat v. Republic of Argentina*, ICSID Case No. ARB/07/5, Procedural Order No. 13 (Sept. 27, 2012), para. 39 (stating that an "Arbitral Tribunal can in principle not prohibit a Party from conducting criminal court proceedings before competent state authorities.").

27 *Caratube International Oil Company LLP v. Republic of Kazakhstan*, ICSID Case No. ARB/08/12, Decision Regarding Claimant's Application for Provisional Measures (July 31, 2009), para. 136. See e.g. *Lao Holdings N.V. v. Lao People's Democratic Republic*, ICSID Case No. ARB(AF)/12/26, Ruling on Motion to Amend the Provisional Measures Order (May 30, 2014), para. 22.

> [T]he language authorizing ICSID Tribunals in Article 47 of the Convention and Rule 39 is very broad and does not give any indication that any specific state action must be excluded from the scope of possible provisional measures. Therefore this tribunal does not agree with the strict approach which seems to have been taken by the Tribunal in the SGS decision ...[28]

Although the *Caratube* tribunal was addressing the ICSID Convention here, there is no reason to believe that any other conclusion should prevail where the arbitration is not based on the ICSID Convention. Unless the treaty expressly excludes interim relief in respect of criminal proceedings, the tribunal will be empowered to render any interim relief in relation thereto.

b *The* Prima Facie *Jurisdiction and Admissibility Condition*

There is broad consensus that an investor-State tribunal hearing a request for interim relief need only be satisfied on a *prima facie* basis that it has jurisdiction over the dispute.[29] This echoes the approach of the ICJ under Article 41[30] as well as the approach in international arbitration.[31] While the discussion in the literature has largely centered on *prima facie* **jurisdiction**, there is obviously no reason why a tribunal should not satisfy itself that claims are *prima facie* **admissible** as well.[32]

---

28 *Caratube International Oil Company LLP v. Republic of Kazakhstan*, ICSID Case No. ARB/08/12, Decision Regarding Claimant's Application for Provisional Measures (July 31, 2009), para. 136. See also *Gerald International v. Sierra Leone*, ICSID Case No. ARB/19/31, Procedural Order No. 2: Decision on the Claimant's Request for Provisional Measures (July 28, 2020), para. 141 ("The BIT is silent on the matter and thus in no way restricts or conditions the Tribunal's power to recommend provisional measures.").

29 See e.g. C. Schreuer, THE ICSD CONVENTION: A COMMENTARY : A COMMENTARY ON THE CONVENTION ON THE SETTLEMENT OF INVESTMENT DISPUTES BETWEEN STATES AND NATIONALS OF OTHER STATES (2009), p. 775; *Quiborax S.A., Non Metallic Minerals S.A. and Allan Fosk Kaplún v. Plurinational State of Bolivia*, ICSID Case No. ARB/06/2, Decision on Provisional Measures (Feb. 26, 2010), para. 108; *PNG Sustainable Development Program Ltd. V. Independent State of Papua New Guinea*, ICSID Case No. ARB/13/33 (Jan. 21, 2015), para. 119; *Hydro S.r.l. and others v. Republic of Albania*, ICSID Case No. ARB/15/28, Order on Provisional Measures (Mar. 3, 2016), para. 3.8.

30 *LaGrand (Germany v United States)*, [1999] ICJ Rep 9 (Mar. 3, 1999).

31 G. Born, INTERNATIONAL COMMERCIAL ARBITRATION (3rd ed., Kluwer, 2020), Chapter 17: Provisional Relief in International Arbitration.

32 *See* Z. Douglas, The INTERNATIONAL LAW OF INVESTMENT CLAIMS (Cambridge University Press, 2010), para. 874.

The reason behind the *prima facie* test is simple: the urgency of the request outweighs the interest in a full review of jurisdiction despite the concern that the tribunal may illegitimately encroach on State sovereignty by ordering interim relief only to find that it does not have jurisdiction (which, to the author's knowledge, no tribunal has done). As Professor Schreuer explained:

> Giving priority to a request for provisional measures means that it has to take precedence over any other issues pending before the tribunal. Where a party has raised jurisdictional objections, the tribunal may have to decide on provisional measures before having ruled on its own jurisdiction. As a consequence, a party may be exposed to provisional measures even though it contests the jurisdiction of an ICSID tribunal. On the other hand, the urgency of the matter often makes it impossible to defer provisional measures until the tribunal's jurisdiction has been fully argued and decided.[33]

What precisely a "*prima facie*" analysis entails, however, has been cause for greater debate.

Many tribunals have offered little more than the pithy conclusion that they have jurisdiction without any analysis. For example, the *City Oriente* tribunal (Professor Juan Fernández-Armesto (chair), Dr. Horacio Grigera Naón, and Professor J. Christopher Thomas QC) stated—without any further analysis:

> Irrespective of Respondents' right, which is still valid, to raise an objection to jurisdiction at some point in the future, the fact remains that, at least on a prima facie basis and without prejudging its decision, it is the Tribunal's view that, should such an objection be raised, the Tribunal has jurisdiction to make this decision.[34]

The dearth of analysis, no doubt, is the product of the timing of many interim measures applications which come towards the start of the proceedings and before any objections to jurisdiction have been fully ventilated. For example, in *City Oriente*, the request came only a year after the request for arbitration

33 *See* C. Schreuer, *The ICSID Convention: A Commentary : a Commentary on the Convention on the Settlement of Investment Disputes between States and Nationals of Other States* (2009), p. 771.

34 *City Oriente Limited v. Republic of Ecuador and Empresa Estatal Petróleos del Ecuador (Petroecuador)* [*I*], ICSID Case No. ARB/06/21, Decision on Provisional Measures (Nov. 19, 2007), para. 50.

was filed before any memorial on the merits (or objections to jurisdiction) had apparently been submitted.[35]

The consensus of numerous tribunals that have entered into further analysis, however, is that the test lies somewhere between an initial review to ensure that the basis for jurisdiction is not merely a frivolous one and a full review of jurisdiction. Those tribunals have explained that this "*prima facie*" analysis requires the tribunal to assess its jurisdiction on the assumption that the facts as pled by the claimant are true.[36] The *Millicom* tribunal (Professor Pierre Tercier (chair), Judge Ronny Abraham, Professor Kaj Hobér) explained that "it is necessary and sufficient that the facts alleged by the applicant establish this jurisdiction without it being necessary or possible at this stage to verify them and analyze them in depth."[37] This was echoed by the *Caratube* tribunal, which explained that "the applicant's burden of proof is that it must establish the requirements with sufficient likelihood, without however having to actually prove the facts underlying them."[38] More recently, the *Gerald International* tribunal (Professor Dr. August Reinisch (chair), Professor Dr. Guido Santiago Tawil, Olufunke Adekoya) explained that "it is necessary and sufficient that the facts alleged by the Claimant establish this jurisdiction without it being necessary or possible at this stage to verify them and analyse them in depth."[39]

While some respondent States have relied on the *Perenco* decision (which did not touch upon criminal proceedings) to argue that a "slower" approach is merited where the respondent State has made objections to jurisdiction, that approach has been rejected expressly when raised.[40] Nonetheless, where an objection to jurisdiction has been articulated prior to the request for interim

---

35 *City Oriente Limited v. Republic of Ecuador and Empresa Estatal Petróleos del Ecuador (Petroecuador)* [*I*], ICSID Case No. ARB/06/21, Decision on Provisional Measures (Nov. 19, 2007), para. 50.

36 See e.g. *Caratube International Oil Company LLP and Devincci Salah Hourani v. Republic of Kazakhstan*, ICSID Case No. ARB/13/13, Decision on the Claimant's Request for Provisional Measures (Dec. 4, 2014), para. 103.

37 *Millicom International Operations B.V. and Sentel GSM SA v. Republic of Senegal*, Decision on the Application for Provisional Measures (Aug. 24, 2009), para. 42.

38 *Caratube International Oil Company LLP & Mr. Devinvvi Salah Hourani v. Republic of Kazakhstan*, ICSID Case No. ARB/13/13, Decision on the Claimants' Request for Provisional Measures (Dec. 4, 2014).

39 *Gerald International v. Sierra Leone*, ICSID Case No. ARB/19/31, Procedural Order No. 2: Decision on the Claimant's Request for Provisional Measures (July 28, 2020), para. 168.

40 *Caratube International Oil Company LLP and Devincci Salah Hourani v. Republic of Kazakhstan*, ICSID Case No. ARB/13/13, Decision on the Claimant's Request for Provisional Measures, December 4, 2014, para. 108.

relief, tribunals have addressed those objections—albeit on a *prima facie* basis. For example, in *Gerald International*, although, the respondent had disputed the claimant's ownership of an investment as well as the evidentiary value of the documents allegedly showing ownership, the tribunal noted that "at first sight" those documents "appear to confirm the ownership relations."[41]

Where no such objection has made, the tribunal's analysis will hew closer to a cursory review—similar to the ICSID Secretary-General's initial check under ICSID Convention Article 36(3) that the dispute is not manifestly outside of the jurisdiction of ICSID. The *City Oriente* tribunal invoked the Secretary-General's check and noted that it too had verified the validity of the contract in which the arbitration agreement had been found and whose existence and validity had not been challenged:

> It should be noted that ICSID's Secretary-General registered City Oriente's request for arbitration, upon the required conclusion (pursuant to Article 36 (3) of the Convention) that the dispute is not manifestly outside of the Centre's jurisdiction. The Tribunal has verified that the Contract, the existence or validity of which has not been brought into question by either party, contains the parties' submission to ICSID arbitration in clause 20.3.[42]

Tribunals whose authority does not derive from the ICSID Convention have reached the same conclusion. The *Pugachev* tribunal, for example, was "of the view that such assessment does not require it to definitely satisfy itself that it has jurisdiction over the merits of the case. All that is required is that the provisions invoked by Claimant appear, prima facie, to afford a basis to establish jurisdiction."[43]

While giving priority to an in interim relief request over a jurisdictional analysis does result in the risk that the tribunal that restrains a State's sovereign conduct does not have jurisdiction over the merits of the dispute, those risks can be justified.

First, the unique nature of investor-State arbitration is such that—even where a State contests jurisdiction *with respect to a specific investor*, it generally

41 *Gerald International v. Sierra Leone*, ICSID Case No. ARB/19/31, Procedural Order No. 2: Decision on the Claimant's Request for Provisional Measures (July 28, 2020), para. 171.

42 *City Oriente Limited v. Republic of Ecuador and Empresa Estatal Petróleos del Ecuador (Petroecuador)* [*I*], ICSID Case No. ARB/06/21, Decision on Provisional Measures (Nov. 19, 2007), para. 50.

43 *Sergei Viktorovich Pugachev v. Russia*, UNCITRAL, Interim Award (July 7, 2007), para. 306.

does not contest the fact that a standing offer to arbitrate exists (or, in other words, that it is a party to a valid treaty with arbitration provisions).[44] This is far removed from the more common case in commercial arbitration where a party may seek the extension of an arbitration agreement in a contract to a party that is not a signatory to that contract, and thus the existence of any offer to arbitrate is in question. In addition, where the arbitration is an ICSID arbitration, the State has not only made a standing offer under the relevant treaty instrument, but is also a standing party to the ICSID Convention, which, of course, contains Article 47.

Second, numerous investor-State tribunals have recognized that an investor-State tribunal has inherent powers to decide provisional measures.[45] Those powers are "a facet of the tribunal's overall procedural powers and its responsibility for its own process,"[46] not necessarily a product of its jurisdiction to decide the merits of the case. A parallel may be drawn to what has been recognized as the ICJ's incidental jurisdiction—or inherent powers—over procedural and jurisdictional issues, such as provisional measures, as opposed to its jurisdiction over the merits.[47]

c *The Merits Condition*

The likelihood of success on the merits generally plays a role in the test applied to interim measures under domestic law, in international commercial arbitration, and even under international law.[48] Not, however, in investor-State arbitration. Investor-State tribunals have generally found that they are not required "to assess the likely outcome of the arbitration,"[49] (although, in the

44 Of course, of late European States have contested *ratione voluntatis* jurisdiction on the basis of the CJEU's decision in the *Achmea* case. Another exception would be where States claim to have validly denied the benefits of a treaty to an investor.

45 *See e.g. Biwater Gauff (Tanzania) Ltd. v. United Republic of Tanzania*, ICSID Case No. ARB/05/22, Procedural Order No. 3 (Sept. 29, 2006), para. 135; *Libananco Holding Co. Ltd. V. Turkey*, ICSID Case No. ARB/06/8, Preliminary Decision (June 23, 2008), para. 78; *Mohammed Munshi v. Mongolia*, SCC EA 2018/007, Award on Emergency Measures (Feb. 5, 2018), para. 45.

46 *Biwater Gauff (Tanzania) Ltd. v. United Republic of Tanzania*, ICSID Case No. ARB/05/22, Procedural Order No. 3 (Sept. 29, 2006), para. 135.

47 S. Rosenne, THE LAW AND PRACTICE OF THE INTERNATIONAL COURT, (1st edn, Leyden 1965) 423; *Aegean Sea Continental Shelf (Greece v. Turkey)*, [1976] ICJ Rep 3 (Separate Opinion of President Jimenez de Arechaga).

48 See e.g. G. Born, INTERNATIONAL COMMERCIAL ARBITRATION (3rd ed., Kluwer, 2020), Chapter 17: Provisional Relief in International Arbitration.

49 *Nova Group Investments B.V. v. Romania*, ICSID Case No. ARB/16/19, Procedural Order No. 7, March 29, 2017, para. 230.

view of the *Nova* tribunal, a simple confirmation that merits allegations are "not frivolous" was necessary[50] and, in *Pugachev*, the tribunal satisfied itself that there was a *prima facie* basis for the merits of the claimant's claim[51]). Rather, investor-State tribunals require litigants to establish a link between the rights whose protection is sought and the merits of the dispute.[52]

The reasons are as follows. ICSID and other tribunals have looked to the rights whose preservation is sought with interim relief (not necessarily a protection of relief on the merits as may be the case in commercial arbitration). This flows from a unique regime based on the ICJ Statute's Article 41. That provision, like ICSID Convention Article 47, refers to "provisional measures which should be taken **to preserve the respective rights of either party.**"[53] This is in contrast to the general approach in international arbitration which does not contain such a limitation.[54]

Yet, there is a key difference between interim relief in investor-State arbitration and interim relief before other international law bodies, like the ICJ (or even international commercial tribunals). Requests for interim relief before the ICJ will nearly always go to the merits of the dispute. Because of the nature of these treaty instruments, litigants in inter-State arbitration will not be seeking a monetary award. For example, in the *LaGrand* case, Germany sought stay of the execution of two of its nationals in a case where its argument on the merits was that the United States had breached the Vienna Convention on Consular Relations by failing to inform the German nationals of their right to consular assistance.[55] This is important because the test for necessity—which will be discussed in greater detail later in this piece—generally requires a requesting party to show that the harm that will likely be caused without an order for interim relief cannot adequately be repaired with an award for damages. However, claims in investor-State arbitrations generally seek an award for damages—not specific performance. This is for at least two reasons.

50 *Nova Group Investments B.V. v. Romania*, ICSID Case No. ARB/16/19, Procedural Order No. 7, March 29, 2017, para. 229.

51 *Sergei Viktorovich Pugachev v. Russia*, UNCITRAL, Interim Award, July 7, 2007, para. 312.

52 Some tribunals have mentioned a requirement that merits allegations be "*not frivolous*". See e.g. *Nova Group Investments B.V. v. Romania*, ICSID Case No. ARB/16/19, Procedural Order No. 7, March 29, 2017, para. 229.

53 Convention on the Settlement of Investment Disputes Between States and Nationals of Other States (International Centre for Settlement of Investment Disputes [ICSID]) 575 UNTS 159, Article 47.

54 G. Born, INTERNATIONAL COMMERCIAL ARBITRATION (3rd ed., Kluwer, 2020), Chapter 17: Provisional Relief in International Arbitration.

55 *LaGrand (Germany v United States)*, [1999] ICJ Rep 9 (Mar. 3, 1999).

First, the protection under an investment treaty is economic in nature. The State guarantees a certain level of conduct *with respect to an investor's investment*. Where the State's conduct breaches that level of conduct and causes the investor damages, it is only logical that the relief sought should be monetary. This is spelled out in many treaties themselves, which, for example, provide that an expropriation will be legal *so long as* some degree of compensation is paid.

Second, investors will find it far easier to enforce a monetary award than one for specific performance. Because the host State's breach of a treaty takes place within its borders, the only recourse an investor may have to enforce specific performance will be before the host State's own courts. This author is not aware of any specific performance order in an investor-State award that has been enforced in a host State. By contrast, the New York Convention and ICSID Convention both contain robust enforcement regimes for monetary relief, which can be invoked anywhere those treaties are in force.

In light of this reality, the only test that is generally applied requires that the right that the claimant seeks to protect "bears a relation with the dispute" or a "strong linkage" to the merits of dispute.[56]

This articulation, however, flies under false colors. When analyzing this requirement, tribunals have not looked at the link between the *rights* and the merits. After all, procedural rights—such as the right to procedural integrity—will not have any connection to the merits of the dispute. Rather (and logically), it is the link between the *criminal proceedings* or other conduct for which interim relief is sought and the merits that investor-State tribunals examine.

Echoing the language of an earlier decision by the *Maffezini* tribunal, the *Tokios Tokeles* tribunal (Professor Prosper Weil (chair), Piero Bernardini, and Daniel Price) explained:

56 *Occidental Petroleum Corporation and Occidental Exploration and Production Company v Republic of Ecuador*, ICSID Case No. ARB/06/11, Decision on Provisional Measures, (Aug. 17, 2007), para. 118; *Lao Holdings N.V. v. Lao People's Democratic Republic*, ICSID Case No. ARB(AF)/12/26 Ruling on Motion to Amend the Provisional Measures Order (May 30, 2014), para. 11. See e.g. *PNG Sustainable Development Program Ltd. V. Independent State of Papua New Guinea*, ICSID Case No. ARB/13/33 (Jan. 21, 2015), para. 146. While these two phrasings may suggest different tests, this does not appear to be the case. Indeed, the tribunal in *Lao Holding N.V. v. Laos* appeared to use both interchangeably. *Lao Holdings N.V. v. Lao People's Democratic Republic*, ICSID Case No. ARB(AF)/12/26, Ruling on Motion to Amend the Provisional Measures Order (May 30, 2014), paras. 11 and 37.

> A tribunal may order a provisional measure if the actions of the opposing party "relate to the subject matter of the case before the tribunal and not to separate, unrelated issues or extraneous matters."[57]

Here, the factual scenarios analyzed by tribunals fall into four categories.

First, where **the criminal proceedings are the conduct that is alleged to breach the relevant treaty on the merits**, a sufficient nexus exists *de facto*.

This was the case, for example, in *Hydro v. Albania*, where criminal proceedings had not only led to the expropriation of the claimants' investment, but, just days before the Request for Arbitration was filed, also led to arrest warrants issued against several of the claimants.[58] The fact that the criminal proceedings pre-date the commencement of the arbitration will pose no problem to establishing a sufficient link to the arbitration (although it may have an effect on how the tribunal views the *status quo* that may be invoked for interim relief, as explained below).

Second, a sufficient nexus has been found to exist where **criminal proceedings, which post-date the start of the arbitration, are employed to further the conduct that is alleged to be a breach of the relevant treaty.** The criminal proceedings are thus a part of, but not the sole element of, the merits claim. For example, in *Caratube*, a State used a criminal investigation as one reason to justify its termination of a concession agreement.[59]

Third, a sufficient nexus exists where it can be shown that **criminal proceedings, which are unrelated to the investor's claim on the merits, have been commenced as retaliation** for the investor's recourse to arbitration or to gain an upper hand in the arbitration.

The relation to the arbitration may be obvious, or even acknowledged. For example, the criminal investigations in *Teinver* and *Quiborax* sought to substantiate allegations of forgery or invalidity of key documents in the arbitration: respectively, the claimant's power of attorney in the arbitration and meeting minutes relevant to the tribunal's jurisdiction.[60] In the *Quiborax* case,

57 *Tokios Tokelés v. Ukraine*, ICSID Case No. ARB/02/18, Procedural Order No. 3 (Jan. 18, 2005), para. 11.

58 *Hydro S.r.l. and others v. Republic of Albania*, ICSID Case No. ARB/15/28, Order on Provisional Measures (Mar. 3, 2016), para. 2.30.

59 *Caratube International Oil Company LLP & Devincci Salah Hourani v. Republic of Kazakhstan*, ICSID Case No. ARB/13/13, Decision on the Claimants' Request for Provisional Measures (Dec. 4, 2014), p. 9.

60 See e.g. *Teinver S.A., Transportes de Cercanías S.A. and Autobuses Urbanos del Sur S.A. v. Argentine Republic*, ICSID Case No. ARB/09/1, Decision on Provisional Measures (Apr. 8, 2016), para. 181 ("The complaints also make references to one of the Respondent's jurisdictional defences in this arbitration"); Occidental Petroleum Corporation and

the criminal complaint even acknowledged that alleged irregularities were detected "in consideration of" the request for arbitration.[61] The *Quiborax* tribunal (composed of Garbielle Kaufmann-Kohler (chair), Marc Lalonde, and Brigitte Stern) relied on an inter-ministerial memorandum, which recommended that "Bolivia should try to find flaws in Claimants' mining concessions as a defense strategy."[62]

The link may also result from the timing of those proceedings. For example, in *Lao Holdings v. Laos*, the tribunal (Ian Binnie, QC (chair), Professor Bernard Hanotiau, Professor Brigitte Stern) found that a sufficient nexus existed between the arbitration and seemingly unrelated criminal proceedings because of the timing of the criminal proceedings: the State had become aware of facts underlying its criminal allegations years earlier, but did not investigate.[63]

Where the relationship to the arbitration is not obvious, there must be some evidence, as in *Lao Holdings*, that the criminal investigation is linked to the arbitration. Such an element was missing in the *Churchill Mining* case (Professor Gabrielle Kaufmann-Kohler (chair), Michael Hwang, SC, Professor Albert Jan ven den Berg), where the claimant contended that a raid was timed to occur when the claimant's employees were participating in a procedural step in the arbitration, but no further evidence was tendered.[64]

Occidental Exploration and Production Company v. Republic of Ecuador, ICSID Case No. ARB/06/11, Decision on Provisional Measures (Aug. 17, 2007), paras. 120 ("the criminal proceedings were initiated as a result of a corporate audit that targeted Claimants *because* they had initiated this arbitration") and 164 ("Although Bolivia may have reasons to suspect that the persons being prosecuted could have engaged in criminal conduct, the facts presented to the Tribunal suggest that the underlying motivation to initiate the criminal proceedings was their connection to this arbitration, which has been expressly deemed to constitute the harm caused to Bolivia that is required as one of the constituent elements of the crimes prosecuted.").

61 *Occidental Petroleum Corporation and Occidental Exploration and Production Company v Republic of Ecuador*, ICSID Case No. ARB/06/11, Decision on Provisional Measures (Aug. 17, 2007), para. 121.

62 *Quiborax S.A., Non Metallic Minerals S.A. and Allan Fosk Kaplún v. Plurinational State of Bolivia*, ICSID Case No. ARB/06/2, Decision on Provisional Measures (Feb. 26, 2010), para. 122.

63 *Lao Holdings N.V. v. Lao People's Democratic Republic*, ICSID Case No. ARB(AF)/12/26, Ruling on Motion to Amend the Provisional Measures Order (May 30, 2014), paras. 37 and 58.

64 *Churchill Mining PLC v. Republic of Indonesia*, ICSID Case No. ARB/12/14, Procedural Order No. 3 (Mar. 4, 2013), para. 86 ("While it is true that the timing of the raid is remarkable, the Tribunal fails to discern an element allowing it to connect the raid to the latest developments in these proceedings. There is certainly an inherent element of disruption with police raids, as they are usually conducted without prior notice. This

Absent such a link, however, there is no nexus and no justification for an interim measure. As the *Hydro* tribunal explained, "there may be situations where incarceration of a claimant would disrupt an arbitration but where it would be improper for the tribunal to intervene," for example, "where a person is charged with a serious offence totally unrelated to the factual circumstances of the dispute being arbitrated, such as murder."[65]

Fourth, where the State is a party **to criminal proceedings in another State,** it must also be shown that it is using its status in bad faith. In *Caratube II* (Laurent Lévy (chair), Laurent Aynès, Jacques Salès), even though the tribunal had "doubts" about the respondent State's "standing and motivation" in criminal proceedings in a third State, it rejected any connection with the arbitration because there was no evidence that the respondent State was using its status as *partie civile* to "pursue its own objectives."[66]

II Protected Rights

> Let us haste to hear it,
> And call the noblest to the audience.
> For me, with sorrow I embrace my fortune.
> I have some rights of memory in this kingdom
> Which now, to claim my vantage doth invite me.
>
> W. SHAKESPEARE, Hamlet, *lns. 4055–4058*

As noted, the ICSID Convention's ICJ heritage compels ICSID litigants to establish rights whose protection merits interim relief. While the reference to the preservation of rights, as we have seen, is specific to the ICSID Convention, it has been echoed by parties and tribunals litigating under other arbitral rules.[67]

---

being so, the Claimants do not allege that the police raided was conducted in breach of Indonesian law.").

65 *Hydro S.r.l. and others v. Republic of Albania*, ICSID Case No. ARB/15/28, Order on Provisional Measures (Mar. 3, 2016), para. 3.19.

66 *Caratube International Oil Company LLP and Devincci Salah Hourani v. Republic of Kazakhstan*, ICSID Case No. ARB/13/13, Decision on the Claimant's Request for Provisional Measures (Dec. 4, 2014), para. 137. See also, *id.* para. 140.

67 See e.g. *Maria Lazareva v. Kuwait*, UNCITRAL, Claimant's Application for Interim Measures under Article 26(1) (Mar. 27, 2019), Section V; *OOO Manolium-Processing v. Belarus*, UNCITRAL, Decision on Claimant's Interim Measures Request (Dec. 1, 2018), Section IV(D); *Sergei Viktorovich Pugachev v. Russia*, UNCITRAL, Interim Award (Jul. 7, 2007), para. 312.

Three rights have generally been invoked by parties seeking an interim measure in relation to criminal proceedings: a right to exclusivity (**a**), a right to non-aggravation and preservation of the *status quo* (**b**), and a right to the procedural integrity of the proceedings (**c**).

a *No Right to Exclusivity*

The right to exclusivity is a creature of ICSID Convention's Article 26, which reads:

> Consent of the parties to arbitration under this Convention shall, unless otherwise stated, be deemed consent to such arbitration to the exclusion of any other remedy. A Contracting State may require the exhaustion of local administrative or judicial remedies as a condition of its consent to arbitration under this Convention.[68]

While the second sentence of Article 26 refers to an "exhaustion of local remedies" requirement as a precondition to valid consent, the first sentence is a two-way street. It prevents any party (State or investor) from commencing proceedings seeking the same remedy before another forum.

Article 26, no doubt, is a broad provision. It has been invoked to order a stay of pending civil, administrative, and bankruptcy proceedings.[69] But is it broad enough to catch even interim measures in relation to criminal proceedings, whose penal objectives are far removed from the monetary objectives of an investor-State arbitration?

One tribunal answered this question in the affirmative. In the 2003 *Tokios Tokéles* decision, a tribunal cast a broad gloss on Article 26 without little analysis of the underlying facts. It explained:

> In becoming a party to the Convention, Ukraine has committed itself to the principle of exclusivity of ICSID proceedings, and, hence, to the exclusion of domestic judicial or administrative remedies. Pursuant to this principle, which lies at the very heart of the ICSID institution and

68 Convention on the Settlement of Investment Disputes Between States and Nationals of Other States (International Centre for Settlement of Investment Disputes [ICSID]) 575 UNTS 159 (1966), Art. 26.

69 *See e.g. Ceskoslovenska Obchodni Banka, A.S. v. The Slovak Republic*, ICSID Case No. ARB/97/4, Procedural Order No. 2, (Sept. 9, 1998); *Perenco Ecuador Ltd. v. Republic of Ecuador and Empresa Estatal Petróleos del Ecuador (Petroecuador)*, ICSID Case No. ARB/08/6, Decision on Provisional Measures (May 8, 2009).

> mechanism, once the parties have consented to ICSID arbitration, they must refrain from initiating or pursuing proceedings in any other forum in respect of the subject matter of the dispute before ICSID.[70]

However, the majority of tribunals have rejected the right to exclusivity as a valid right whose protection may lead to interim measures in relation to criminal proceedings. In *Quiborax*, for example, the tribunal explained that a right to exclusivity only covers investment disputes:

> The question that arises is whether the continuation of the criminal proceedings referred to in this decision threatens the exclusivity of the ICSID proceedings. The Tribunal considers that it does not. Although it finds that the criminal proceedings are related to the ICSID arbitration, that does not per se threaten the exclusivity of the arbitration proceedings under Article 26 of the ICSID Convention. Pursuant to Article 25 of the ICSID Convention, the Centre has jurisdiction to resolve investment disputes. Thus, the exclusivity of the ICSID proceedings applies only to investment disputes, i.e. here to the determination of whether Respondent has breached its international obligations under the BIT and whether Claimants are entitled to the relief they seek.[71]

Thus, the *Lao Holding* tribunal explained that Article 46 "applies only to civil proceedings having the same parties and same subject matter as the arbitral proceeding and does not concern criminal procedures."[72]

b *The Right to Non-Aggravation of the Dispute and Preservation of the* Status Quo

The right to non-aggravation of the dispute and preservation of the status quo is a result of the ICSID regime's ICJ heritage. While the ICJ Statute makes no mention of any such right, the treaties that predate the Statute—such as the 1902 Treaty of Corinto—referred to a similar obligation (for example, "not to

---

70 *Tokios Tokelés v. Ukraine*, ICSID Case No. ARB/02/18, Procedural Order No. 1 (July 1, 2003), para. 1; *Tokios Tokelés v. Ukraine*, ICSID Case No. ARB/02/18, Procedural Order No. 3 (Jan. 18, 2005), para. 7.

71 *Quiborax S.A., Non Metallic Minerals S.A. and Allan Fosk Kaplún v. Plurinational State of Bolivia*, ICSID Case No. ARB/06/2, Decision on Provisional Measures (Feb. 26, 2010), para. 128.

72 *Lao Holdings N.V. v. Lao People's Democratic Republic*, ICSID Case No. ARB(AF)/12/26, Ruling on Motion to Amend the Provisional Measures Order (May 30, 2014), para. 21.

execute any act of hostilities, preparations for war, or mobilization of forces, in order to impede the settlement of the difficulty or question by the means established in the present convention").[73] The PCIJ's *Electricity Company* decision became the first international law decision to recognize such a right independent of any treaty text. It acknowledged a "principle universally accepted by international tribunals and likewise laid down in many conventions to which Bulgaria has been a party-to the effect that the parties to a case must abstain from any measure capable of exercising a prejudicial effect in regard to the execution of the decision to be given and, in general, not allow any step of any kind to be taken which might aggravate or extend the dispute."[74] Subsequent ICJ decisions have echoed this right.[75]

The experience of investor-State tribunals has followed a similar path. During the drafting of the ICSID Convention, Spain's delegate even suggested that Article 47 expressly state that "none of the parties will take any action during proceedings which might impede the normal execution of the award,"[76] but that suggestion was not adopted. In the absence of any express provision, however, tribunals have followed ICJ case law. The 2006 decision by the *Biwater* tribunal (Bernard Hanotiau (chair), Toby Landau QC, Gary Born), for example, considered such a right "now settled in both treaty and international commercial arbitration."[77] Since that decision, numerous tribunals have recognized such a right in respect to interim measures, including, in relation to criminal proceedings.[78]

The case law in relation to this right merits three observations.

---

73 *See* C. Miles, PROVISIONAL MEASURES BEFORE INTERNATIONAL COURTS AND TRIBUNALS (Cambridge University Press, 2017), Chapter 2: Origins of Provisional Matters.

74 *The Electricity Company of Sofia and Bulgaria (Belgium v. Bulgaria)*, 1939 P.C.I.J. (ser. A/B) No. 77 (Apr. 4, 1939).

75 *See e.g. Case of Certain Criminal Proceedings in France (France v. Congo)*, [2003] I.C.J. Rep., 102, 111 (Jun. 17, 2003).

76 THE HISTORY OF THE ICSID CONVENTION: VOLUME II (1970), p. 814 [available at https://icsid.worldbank.org/resources/publications/the-history-of-the-icsid-convention] (last visited on April 4, 2021).

77 *Biwater Gauff (Tanzania) Ltd. v. United Republic of Tanzania*, ICSID Case No. ARB/05/22, Procedural Order No. 3 (Sept. 29, 2006), para. 135.

78 *See e.g. Italba Corporation v. Oriental Republic of* Uruquay, ICSID Case No. ARB/16/9, Decision on Claimant's Application for Provisional Measures and Temporary Relief (Feb. 15, 2017), para. 118; *Hydro S.r.l. and others v. Republic of Albania*, ICSID Case No. ARB/15/28, Order on Provisional Measures (Mar. 3, 2016), para. 4.3; *Ipek Investment Limited v. Republic of Turkey*, ICSID Case No. ARB/18/18, Procedural Order No. 5, (Sept. 19, 2019), para. 4.3.

First, as to its nature: the right to non-aggravation and preservation of the *status quo* require some nexus between the criminal proceedings and the arbitration, even if the subject matter of the two proceedings is not the same. As explained by the *Convial Callao* tribunal composed of Yves Derains (chair), Brigitte Stern, and Eduardo Zuleta, the mere opening of a criminal proceeding does not modify the *status quo*.[79] In order to rely on the right of non-aggravation, the *Quiborax* tribunal established that "although the criminal proceedings do not deal with the same subject matter as the ICSID proceeding, they are sufficiently related to merit the protection of Claimants' rights to the non-aggravation of the dispute and the preservation of the status quo, which the Tribunal considers to be self-standing rights."[80] In that case, the mere fact that the proceedings "exacerbate the climate of hostility" was sufficient.[81] However, more recent cases appear to fold the right of non-aggravation in with the right to procedural integrity. Regarding preservation of the *status quo*, for example, the *Ipek* tribunal stated:

> The Tribunal is not concerned with the pendency of criminal charges against the Targeted Individuals. It is concerned solely with steps that may be taken subsequent to its Order that may affect the fairness of its procedure.[82]

This conclusion is not consistent with prior law. It would suggest that the right of non-aggravation is not substantially different from the right to procedural integrity. If that were true, it would mean that the right of non-aggravation would have a bespoke meaning in relation to pending criminal proceedings (rather than, for example, insolvency, tax or any other proceedings), and seems unlikely.

Second, as to the relevant timing of a request seeking protection of the right to non-aggravation: if the investment has already been expropriated

---

79 *Convial Callao S.A. and CCI—Compañia de Concesiones de Infraestructura S.A. v. Peru*, Decisión sobre Solicitud de Medidas Provisionales, ICSID Case No. ARB/10/2 (Feb. 22, 2011), para. 103.

80 *Quiborax S.A., Non Metallic Minerals S.A. and Allan Fosk Kaplún v. Plurinational State of Bolivia*, ICSID Case No. ARB/06/2, Decision on Provisional Measures (Feb. 26, 2010), para. 133.

81 *Quiborax S.A., Non Metallic Minerals S.A. and Allan Fosk Kaplún v. Plurinational State of Bolivia*, ICSID Case No. ARB/06/2, Decision on Provisional Measures (Feb. 26, 2010), para. 138.

82 *Ipek Investment Limited v. Republic of Turkey*, ICSID Case No. ARB/18/18, Procedural Order No. 5 (Sept. 19, 2019), para. 60.

and investment activity has ceased when the request for arbitration is filed, criminal proceedings cannot threaten the *status quo* (unlike, for example, procedural integrity, which can be threatened in such cases). This was the finding of the *Quiborax* tribunal:

> The Tribunal agrees with Claimants that the criminal proceedings exacerbate the climate of hostility in which the dispute is unfolding. However, it also notes that Claimants have no more activities or presence in Bolivia. Their mining concessions have been revoked, so there is no ongoing investment to protect. Co-Claimant Allan Fosk—the only Claimant implicated in the criminal proceedings—has not been formally accused and does not live in Bolivia. Thus, the Tribunal cannot agree with Claimants that the criminal proceedings place "intolerable pressure" on Claimants to drop their claims. Likewise, the Tribunal cannot concur with Claimants" argument that the criminal proceedings have changed the status quo of the dispute because they have turned them into defendants in Bolivia. If there are legitimate grounds for the criminal proceedings, Claimants must bear the burden of their conduct in Bolivia.[83]

Likewise, in the *Nova* case, the tribunal expressly rejected the suggestion that criminal proceedings must post-date the commencement of the arbitration **and** must be aimed at thwarting the arbitration.[84] It found that "[w]here the right is only the preservation of the *status quo*, an inquiry into the timing is inherent; the tribunal must first identify the *status quo* in order to determine whether it should be preserved, and the *status quo* may reflect the fact that criminal proceedings already are underway."[85]

The conclusion may be a different one—as the *Nova* tribunal explained—where the right is one of procedural integrity: "The fact that the arbitration may have been filed after the domestic criminal proceedings, rather than before, does not deprive the investor of its basic right to be heard."[86]

---

83 *Quiborax S.A., Non Metallic Minerals S.A. and Allan Fosk Kaplún v. Plurinational State of Bolivia*, ICSID Case No. ARB/06/2, Decision on Provisional Measures (Feb. 26, 2010), para. 138.

84 *Nova Group Investments B.V. v. Romania*, ICSID Case No. ARB/16/19, Procedural Order No. 7 (Mar. 29, 2017), paras. 249–257.

85 *Nova Group Investments B.V. v. Romania*, ICSID Case No. ARB/16/19, Procedural Order No. 7 (Mar. 29, 2017), para. 254.

86 *Nova Group Investments B.V. v. Romania*, ICSID Case No. ARB/16/19, Procedural Order No. 7 (Mar. 29, 2017), para. 255.

Third, as to the content of the right to non-aggravation: a party's obligation to conduct arbitral proceedings in good faith requires that it not take any actions that would unnecessarily aggravate the dispute[87] once the request for arbitration has been filed.[88] It results from the "principle that in the course of litigation the parties must refrain from taking steps that might affect the rights of the other side which are the object of the proceedings on the merits."[89] One ICSID tribunal has defined this right as protecting against "actions which would make resolution of the dispute by the Tribunal more difficult" where "a change of circumstances threatens the ability of the Arbitral Tribunal to grant the relief which a party seeks and the capability of giving effect to the relief."[90] The right to non-aggravation does not imply a "sweeping right to freeze all circumstances as they then exist" and, therefore, does not allow a claimant to put a halt to conduct that began *before* the arbitration commenced.[91] Rather, it is designed to prevent a party from taking *new* action that is not conducive to resolution of the dispute. In the *City Oriente* case, for example, the tribunal issued an interim order to halt a criminal investigation into officers of the respondent on the allegation that they had failed to make payment of an amount in dispute in the ICSID proceedings, concluding that these proceedings

87 *Caratube International Oil Company LLP v. Republic of Kazakhstan*, ICSID Case No. ARB/08/12, Decision Regarding Claimant's Application for Provisional Measures (July 31, 2009), para. 115 (referring to a "general duty, arising from the principle of good faith, not to take any action that may aggravate the dispute or affect the integrity of the arbitration").; *Lao Holdings N.V. v. Lao People's Democratic Republic*, ICSID Case No. ARB(AF)/12/26, Ruling on Motion to Amend the Provisional Measures Order (May 30, 2014), para. 15.

88 It bears noting that the relevant "status quo" for the purpose of this right is the request for arbitration, although some tribunals have been willing to accept some leeway. This makes sense as a long notice period may allow the respondent to unfairly take measures that aggravate the dispute. See *Sergei Viktorovich Pugachev v. Russia*, UNCITRAL, Interim Award 5July 7, 2007°, para. 290 ("In Hydro v. Albania, claimants were not formally notified of any criminal proceedings against them, and their arrest warrants were issued less than one week before the initiation of the arbitration").

89 C. Schreuer, The ICSID Convention: A Commentary : a Commentary on the Convention on the Settlement of Investment Disputes between States and Nationals of Other States (2009), pp. 797–798.

90 *Plama Consortium Limited v. Republic of Bulgaria*, ICSID Case No. ARB/03/24, Order (Sept. 6, 2005), para. 45.

91 *Nova Group Investments B.V. v. Romania*, ICSID Case No. ARB/16/19, Procedural Order No. 7 (March 29, 2017), para. 236.

were opened "as a means to coactively secure payment of amounts allegedly owed."[92]

Unlike the right to procedural integrity, the right to non-aggravation can be invoked in support of a measure that protects the claimant's investment. However, this right is not a shield against *any* State action. An investor must prove that it has something substantive to protect. It cannot claim compensation for expropriation in ICSID arbitration while seeking to prevent a State from using its criminal law police powers to divest the claimant of that same investment.[93] Likewise, the right to non-aggravation cannot lead to interim relief in respect to every circumstance where the claimant's loss is simply "more damages."[94] Instead, it protects the investor from the situation in which the other party takes justice into its own hands, thereby undermining the role of the arbitrators in resolving the dispute.[95] For example, where the parties have

---

92 *City Oriente Limited v. Republic of Ecuador*, ICSID Case No. ARB/06/21, Decision on Provisional Measures (Nov. 19, 2007), para. 63.

93 *Quiborax S.A., Non Metallic Minerals S.A. and Allan Fosk Kaplún v. Plurinational State of Bolivia*, ICSID Case No. ARB/06/2, Decision on Provisional Measures (Feb. 26, 2010), para. 138 ("The Tribunal agrees with Claimants that he criminal proceedings exacerbate the climate of hostility in in which the dispute is unfolding. However, it also notes that Claimants have no more activities or presence in Bolivia [...] the Tribunal cannot concur with Claimants' argument that the criminal proceedings have changed the *status quo* of the dispute because they have turned them into defendants in Bolivia. If there are legitimate grounds for the criminal proceedings, Claimants must bear the burden of their conduct in Bolivia"). See also *Teinver S.A., Transportes de Cercanías S.A. and Autobuses Urbanos del Sur S.A. v. Argentine Republic*, ICSID Case No. ARB/09/1, Decision on Provisional Measures (Apr. 8, 2016), para. 199 ("Claimants have not specified how the *status quo* of their investment in Argentina would be affected by the criminal proceedings. The Argentine Airlines in which Claimants held their disputed investment has been expropriated for some time now and there was no indication how the criminal proceedings would affect this or otherwise affect the *status quo*.").

94 *Occidental Petroleum Corporation and Occidental Exploration and Production Company v Republic of Ecuador*, ICSID Case No. ARB/06/11, Decision on Provisional Measures (Aug. 17, 2007), para. 99 ("The harm in this case is only 'more damages' and this is harm of a type which can be compensated by monetary compensation, so there is neither necessity nor urgency to grant a provisional measure to prevent such harm.").

95 *Occidental Petroleum Corporation and Occidental Exploration and Production Company v Republic of Ecuador*, ICSID Case No. ARB/06/11, Decision on Provisional Measures (Aug. 17, 2007), para. 97 ("provisional measure, when granted as measures required to prevent aggravation of the dispute, have always been directed at the behavior of the parties to the dispute , whether they consisted of measures required to maintain—or restore—peace between them, or to prevent one party from initiating or pursuing parallel litigation, for example in the national courts, thereby directly undermining the international proceedings. Provisional measures are not designed to merely mitigate

an ongoing relationship of cooperation, the right to non-aggravation would prevent the host State from taking any new action after the request for arbitration is filed that would render meaningless a claim for specific performance or could put an end to the relationship.[96] The extent to which an ICSID tribunal will go to protect a party's right to non-aggravation will depend on what the tribunal considers "necessary" to protect that right, as discussed below.

c *The Right to Procedural Integrity*

The right to procedural integrity is procedural in nature (as its name suggests).[97] Unlike the right to non-aggravation, it has nothing to do with the merits, but rather the claimant's ability to put on its case. Thus, for example, where criminal proceedings both aggravate the dispute (potentially leading to irreparable damage to an investment) and also threaten the procedural integrity of the arbitration (thus potentially leading to irreparable damage to the arbitration), a claimant may seek provisional measures on grounds that the measures are necessary to protect both the right to non-aggravation and procedural integrity. The tribunal's approach to the question of whether a provisional measures order is merited will differ depending on the right in question.

The right to procedural integrity, according to the case law, has two manifestations.

First, the right to procedural integrity protects a party's due process rights in the arbitration. Thus, interim relief has been granted to protect this right and

---

the final amount of damages."). *But see City Oriente Limited v. Republic of Ecuador*, ICSID Case No. ARB/06/21, Decision on Provisional Measures (Nov. 19, 2007), para. 55 ("it is the Tribunal's view that Article 47 of the Convention provides authorization for the passing of provisional measures prohibiting any action that affects the disputed rights, aggravates the dispute, frustrates the effectiveness of the award or entails having either party take justice into their own hands").

96 *Burlington Resources Inc. and Others v. Republic of Ecuador and Empresa Estatal Petroleos del Ecuador*, ICSID Case No. ARB/08/5, Procedural Order No. 1 (June 29, 2009), paras. 65, 67, and 68 ("There is no doubt in the Tribunal's mind that the seizures of the oil production decided in the coactiva proceedings are bound to aggravate the present dispute [...] the status quo at issue, the one that needs protection [...] consists in the continuation of the cooperation between the Parties in the framework of the PSCs [...] the Tribunal holds that Burlington Oriente has shown the existence of a right to preservation of the status quo and the non-aggravation of the dispute.").

97 *Nova Group Investments B.V. v. Romania*, ICSID Case No. ARB/16/19, Procedural Order No. 7 (Mar. 29, 2017), para. 235; *Plama Consortium Limited v. Republic of Bulgaria*, ICSID Case No. ARB/03/24, Order (Sept. 6, 2005), para. 40.

prevent the respondent State from depriving the claimant of documentary[98] or witness[99] evidence or access to a party representative,[100] using a criminal investigation to collect evidence for the arbitration that would violate the equality of the parties,[101] or threatening the claimants' counsel.[102]

---

98 *Occidental Petroleum Corporation and Occidental Exploration and Production Company v Republic of Ecuador*, ICSID Case No. ARB/06/11, Decision on Provisional Measures (Aug. 17, 2007), para. 139.

99 This may occur where the criminal proceedings create a chilling effect on obtaining witness evidence. *Occidental Petroleum Corporation and Occidental Exploration and Production Company v Republic of Ecuador*, ICSID Case No. ARB/06/11, Decision on Provisional Measures (Aug. 17, 2007), para. 142 ("Even if no undue pressure is exercised on potential witnesses, the very nature of these criminal proceedings is bound to reduce their willingness to cooperate in the ICSID proceeding. Given that the existence of this ICSID arbitration has been characterized within the criminal proceedings as a harm to Bolivia, it is unlikely that the persons charged will feel free to participate as witnesses in this arbitration."). *But see Churchill Mining PLC v. Republic of Indonesia*, ICSID Case No. ARB/12/14, Procedural Order No. 3 (Mar. 4, 2013), para. 87 ("Again without any concrete element of intimidation, harassment or otherwise abusive behavior, and failing evidence from any potential witnesses, the present situation does not suffice to justify provisional measures. In this sense, Quiborax must be distinguished to the extent that it involved a concrete case of intimidation of one of the claimant's witnesses that had been silenced and prevented from testifying in favor of the claimants in the arbitration. There is no trace of such abusive behavior in the present case.").

100 *Hydro S.r.l. and others v. Republic of Albania*, ICSID Case No. ARB/15/28, Order on Provisional Measures (Mar. 3, 2016), para. 3.18 ("In the case of Mr Becchetti (and Mr De Renzis), who face extradition from the United Kingdom as a result of the arrest warrants, their possible incarceration in Albania would prevent them from effectively managing their businesses, and fully participating in this arbitration. The Tribunal considers that this is a grave concern to the procedural integrity of the proceeding."); *Nova Group Investments B.V. v. Romania*, ICSID Case No. ARB/16/19, Procedural Order No. 7 (Mar. 29, 2017), para. 307 ("It is not credible that [*Mr Adamescu*] could perform this outreach to potential witnesses from behind bars").

101 *Lao Holdings N.V. v. Lao People's Democratic Republic*, ICSID Case No. ARB(AF)/12/26, Ruling on Motion to Amend the Provisional Measures Order (May 30, 2014), para. 26 ("there are however, a number of exceptional circumstances in this case which lead the Tribunal to depart from the general rule entitling a State to enforce on the national level its criminal laws. In particular, the tribunal is satisfied on the evidence that the primary purpose for which the Respondent intends to use the powers of criminal investigation, at least in the first instance, is to collect evidence for use at the arbitration, which, in the result, will undermine the integrity of arbitral processed.").

102 *Teinver S.A., Transportes de Cercanías S.A. and Autobuses Urbanos del Sur S.A. v. Argentine Republic*, ICSID Case No. ARB/09/1, Decision on Provisional Measures (Apr. 8, 2016), para. 205 ("In the Tribunal's view the threat of criminal proceedings against counsel in the circumstances of this case places substantial pressure on counsel. This, in turn, threatens to affect Claimants' right to be represented by counsel of their choice in this arbitration").

In *Quiborax*, for example, the tribunal invoked the procedural right to access to evidence and a potential chilling effect on witnesses.[103] In *Hydro*, the tribunal stated axiomatically that an award could not compensate the claimants if they were effectively prevented from participating in the arbitration:

> Whilst the destruction of the Claimants' investments in Albania may be capable of being repaired by an award of damages as the Respondent points out, the Claimants' ability to effectively participate in the arbitration, by definition, cannot be adequately remedied by damages.[104]

Some tribunals, however, have approached the substance of procedural rights with broader brush strokes. In *Caratube*, for example, the tribunal identified as procedural rights that could be protected by interim measures (i) the claimant's "right to avoid further exposure to or responsibility for potential economic or ecological damage in the Contract Area, and other uncertainty, risk and responsibility (including further financial exposure) associated with its continued custody of the Contract Area, which may aggravate the dispute"; (ii) its "right to pursue its claims in this arbitration without risk of being beholden to Kazakh authorities in such a manner that may aggravate the dispute"; (iii) its "right to pursue its claims in this arbitration in an orderly fashion without risk that CIOC or its employees are exposed to the risk of further sanctions or harassment relating to its dispute with Kazakhstan"; and (iv) the more traditional right of the claimant "to have access to its documents and materials."[105]

Finally, it bears noting that timing may also be relevant to an application for interim measures related to procedural integrity. The *Teinver* tribunal found that the fact that criminal proceedings had been commenced after the hearing on the merits where the only remaining steps were the closure of the arbitration and issuance of the award "reduces the aspects of the arbitration in respect of which provisional measures can be sought."[106]

---

103 *Quiborax S.A., Non Metallic Minerals S.A. and Allan Fosk Kaplún v. Plurinational State of Bolivia*, ICSID Case No. ARB/06/2, Decision on Provisional Measures (Feb. 26, 2010), paras. 142–148.

104 Hydro S.r.l. and others v. Republic of Albania, ICSID Case No. ARB/15/28, Order on Provisional Measures (Mar. 3, 2016), para. 3.34.

105 *Caratube International Oil Company LLP v. Republic of Kazakhstan*, ICSID Case No. ARB/08/12, Decision Regarding Claimant's Application for Provisional Measures (July 31, 2009), p. 43.

106 *Teinver S.A., Transportes de Cercanías S.A. and Autobuses Urbanos del Sur S.A. v. Argentine Republic*, ICSID Case No. ARB/09/1, Decision on Provisional Measures (Apr. 8, 2016), para. 191.

Second, the right to procedural integrity protects the "right to protection of the effectivity of the award."[107] This does not mean, as does the right to non-aggravation, protection of the substantive rights of the parties, as at least one tribunal has suggested.[108] Rather, it refers to attempts to undermine the jurisdiction of the ICSID tribunal and render an award unenforceable or ineffective. States, for example, have sought to use their criminal investigatory powers to allege that a claimant's consent to arbitration was forged.[109]

Both manifestations of this right ultimately protect the integrity of the arbitral process and, in the context of criminal proceedings, prevent the State from using its superior powers to frustrate the arbitral process. For this reason, unlike the right of non-aggravation, there is no real parallel in the ICJ case law. The right to procedural integrity—after all—is the product of the inherent inequality between the parties in investor-State arbitration.

III Requirements

> The better part of
> valour is discretion; in the which better part I
> have saved my life.
>
> W. SHAKESPEARE, Henry IV, Part I, *lns. 3086–3088*

Neither the ICSID Convention nor any arbitration rules generally applied in investor-State arbitration lay out a discrete test for interim measures. Thus, the determination of any such test, as well as its application, rests within the unfettered discretion of the tribunal. In contrast to the approach that some tribunals have taken to certain terms of the ICSID Convention (for example, the definition of "investment"[110]), tribunals have been largely in lock-step

---

107 *Burlington Resources Inc. and Others v. Republic of Ecuador and Empresa Estatal Petroleos del Ecuador*, ICSID Case No. ARB/08/5, Procedural Order No. 1 (June 29, 2009), para. 61.

108 *Nova Group Investments B.V. v. Romania*, ICSID Case No. ARB/16/19, Procedural Order No. 7 (Mar. 29, 2017), para. 236 ("The Tribunal interprets this narrowly, as relevant primarily in the same context (*i.e.* the impact on the ongoing ICSID proceeding) as the right to procedural integrity addressed above.").

109 *See Teinver S.A., Transportes de Cercanías S.A. and Autobuses Urbanos del Sur S.A. v. Argentine Republic*, ICSID Case No. ARB/09/1, Decision on Provisional Measures (Apr. 8, 2016).

110 *Compare Salini et al v. Morocco*, ICSID Case No. ARB/00/4, Decision on Jurisdiction, July 23, 2001, para. 52 *with Quiborax S.A., Non Metallic Minerals S.A. and Allan Fosk Kaplún v. Plurinational State of Bolivia*, ICSID Case No. ARB/06/2, Decision on Jurisdiction (Sept. 27, 2002), para. 220.

when it comes to the criteria applicable to an interim measures order sought in relation to criminal proceedings. That, no doubt, is because such criteria have been adopted from ICJ case law (and also happen to be present in other legal systems).

At least two requirements must be met for an order of interim relief: necessity (**a**) and urgency (**b**). A third, proportionality, is present in the reasoning of tribunals even where tribunals do not consider it expressly as a separate prong (**c**).

a *Necessity*

Tribunals have grappled with two aspects of the necessity prong.

First, tribunals have looked to the degree of potential harm that would occur in the absence of interim relief.

In the initial decisions, tribunals required "irreparable harm," echoing the case law of the ICJ.[111] For example, in *Tokios Tokelés*, the first public decision to address interim measures in relation to criminal proceedings, the tribunal noted:

> The international jurisprudence on provisional measures indicates that a provisional measure is necessary where the actions of a party "are capable of causing or of threatening irreparable prejudice to the rights invoked."[112]

However, many tribunals have eschewed the "irreparable" harm requirement. In one of the earlier decisions on point from 2008, the *City Oriente* tribunal explained that no irreparable harm requirement could be read into the language of the ICSID Convention and the ICSID Rules:

> It is the opinion of the Tribunal that this wording requires only that provisional measures must not be ordered lightly, but only as a last resort, after careful consideration of the interests at stake, weighing the harm spared the petitioner and the damage inflicted on the other party. It is not so essential that provisional measures be necessary to prevent irreparable harm, but that the harm spared the petitioner by such measures

111 *LaGrand (Germany v United States)*, [1999] ICJ Rep. 9 (Mar. 3, 1999), 15.

112 *Tokios Tokelés v. Ukraine*, ICSID Case No. ARB/02/18, Procedural Order No. 3 (Jan. 18, 2005), para. 8

> must be significant and that it exceed greatly the damage caused to the party affected thereby.[113]

Ultimately, however, the distinction may only be one of semantics. The level of prejudice required appears to turn on the nature of the right invoked, rather than the qualification of the prejudice.

When the interim measure seeks to protect **procedural integrity of the arbitration**, the measure will be necessary by definition because the harm will not only be substantial, but irreparable.[114] After all, it is impossible to quantify the damages resulting from a party's inability to properly participate in the arbitration.

However, the claimant will need to show that—in the words of the *Caratube* tribunal—"its procedural right to continue with this ICSID arbitration is precluded by the criminal investigation"[115] or some other criminal law conduct carried out by the State. In that case, the tribunal found that the claimant had not made such a showing even though a criminal investigation was ongoing, but no arrests had been made and no relevant documents seized. The *Caratube* tribunal *did* suggest that, if the claimant had sought specific performance as relief on the merits, it may have been able to make out a case for necessity, but, as its claim was for damages and, "such damage may be claimed, examined and decided later in the case" and compensated through monetary damages, there was no basis for interim relief.[116]

It bears noting that, in the words of the *Ipek Investment* tribunal, composed of Professor Campbell McLachlan QC (chair), Yves Fortier, QC, and Laurent Lévy, "a tribunal will not exercise its powers in this respect where the alleged risk is only a potential one. It must be imminent."[117] For example, in *OOO Manolium-Processing* and *Pugachev*, tribunals declined to issue a specific order

113 *City Oriente Limited v. Republic of Ecuador and Empresa Estatal Petróleos del Ecuador (Petroecuador)* [*I*], ICSID Case No. ARB/06/21, Decision on Provisional Measures (Nov. 19, 2007), para. 72.

114 *Hydro S.r.l. and others v. Republic of Albania*, ICSID Case No. ARB/15/28, Order on Provisional Measures, March 3, 2016, para. 3.34; *Nova Group Investments B.V. v. Romania*, ICSID Case No. ARB/16/19, Procedural Order No. 7 (Mar. 29, 2017), para. 240.

115 *Caratube International Oil Company LLP v. Republic of Kazakhstan*, ICSID Case No. ARB/08/12, Decision Regarding Claimant's Application for Provisional Measures (July 31, 2009), para. 139.

116 *Caratube International Oil Company LLP v. Republic of Kazakhstan*, ICSID Case No. ARB/08/12, Decision Regarding Claimant's Application for Provisional Measures (July 31, 2009), para. 139.

117 *Ipek Investment Limited v. Republic of Turkey*, ICSID Case No. ARB/18/18, Procedural Order No. 5 (Sept. 19, 2019), para. 43.

in relation to alleged intimidation of witnesses through criminal proceedings that had not yet commenced because no intimidation had been shown.[118]

Where, however, the right is the **right to non-aggravation of the dispute**, two comments are merited.

First, where this right is invoked in relation to the substantive relief sought (e.g. to prevent the State's seizure of assets), the prejudice may nonetheless be irreparable. While the majority of tribunals have referred to irreparable, rather than substantial, harm,[119] several tribunals have nonetheless ordered relief where business interests—which are themselves inherently capable of remedy through monetary damages—were at risk.[120]

This is only logical. If a party could not seek to prevent prejudice that is quantifiable, the right to non-aggravation would be all but ineffective. While a party may not seek protection from "more damages,"[121] tribunals have ordered provisional measures where "the project and its economic standing is at risk

---

118 *OOO Manolium-Processing v. Belarus*, UNCITRAL, Decision on Claimant's Interim Measures Request (Dec. 1, 2018), paras. 59, 123; *Sergei Viktorovich Pugachev v. Russia*, UNCITRAL, Interim Award (July 7, 2007), paras. 345–346.

119 *Quiborax S.A., Non Metallic Minerals S.A. and Allan Fosk Kaplún v. Plurinational State of Bolivia*, ICSID Case No. ARB/06/2, Decision on Provisional Measures (Feb. 26, 2010), para. 156; *Hydro S.r.l. and others v. Republic of Albania*, ICSID Case No. ARB/15/28, Order on Provisional Measures (Mar. 3, 2016), para. 3.16; *Nova Group Investments B.V. v. Romania*, ICSID Case No. ARB/16/19, Procedural Order No. 7 (Mar. 29, 2017), para. 238.

120 *PNG Sustainable Development Program Ltd. V. Independent State of Papua New Guinea*, ICSID Case No. ARB/13/33 (Jan. 21, 2015), para. 109 ("In the Tribunal's view, the term 'irreparable' harm is properly understood as requiring a showing of a material risk of serious or grave damage to the requesting party, and not harm that is literally 'irreparable' in what is sometimes regarded as the narrow common law sense of the term."); *Occidental Petroleum Corporation and Occidental Exploration and Production Company v Republic of Ecuador*, ICSID Case No. ARB/06/11, Decision on Provisional Measures, (Aug. 17, 2007), para. 79 ("Where action by one party may cause loss to the other which may not be capable of being made good by an eventual award of damages, the test in the Article is likely to be met. But the Article does not lay down a test of irreparable loss and the authorities do not warrant so narrow a construction."). *See also Sergei Paushok and others v. Government of Mongolia*, UNCITRAL, Order on Interim Measures, September 2, 2008, para. 69. *But see Nova Group Investments B.V. v. Romania*, ICSID Case No. ARB/16/19, Procedural Order No. 7 (Mar. 29, 2017), para. 337 (noting that the complexity of calculating damages does not mean that the tribunal is unable to craft meaningful damages).

121 *Occidental Petroleum Corporation and Occidental Exploration and Production Company v Republic of Ecuador*, ICSID Case No. ARB/06/11, Decision on Provisional Measures, (Aug. 17, 2007), para. 99 ("The harm in this case is only 'more damages' and this is harm of a type which can be compensated by monetary compensation, so there is neither necessity nor urgency to grant a provisional measure to prevent such harm.")

regardless of the conduct of the investor,"[122] where there is a risk of "destruction of an ongoing investment and of its revenue-producing potential which benefits both the investor and the State"[123] in the words of the *Burlington* tribunal (Profesor Gabrielle Kaufmann Kohler (chair), Profesor Brigitte Stern, Professor Francisco Orrego Vicuña) and the claimant's business in the host State would be "effectively brought to an end" in the words of the *Perenco* tribunal (Lord Bingham of Cornhill (chair), Honourable Judge Charles Brower, Christopher Thomas, QC).[124]

Second, protection of the right to non-aggravation is only triggered in respect to criminal proceedings where there is in an element of bad faith.[125] As the *Gerald International* tribunal explained, "criminal investigations initiated as a retaliation for bringing an investment case, or with a view to intimidating and harassing potential witnesses of a Party may give rise to a situation where provisional measures are exceptionally warranted."[126] Thus, the *Italba* tribunal, comprised of Rodrigo Oreamuno (chair), John Beechey, and Professor Zachary Douglas QC, declined to suspend a criminal investigation because "there is no evidence on the record to support Claimant's contention that the criminal investigation in the present case has been brought in bad faith by the Uruguayan authorities."[127] By contrast, in *City Oriente*, the tribunal ordered the respondent State, Ecuador, to refrain from initiating civil, administrative, and criminal proceedings against the claimant. Although the *City Oriente* tribunal stated that it "has great respect for the Ecuadorian Judiciary" and acknowledged that "Ecuador's sovereign right to prosecute and punish crimes of all kinds perpetrated in its territory," it nonetheless found that "such undisputed right of the Republic of Ecuador should not be used as a means to

---

122 *Burlington Resources Inc. and others v. Republic of Ecuador and Empresa Estatal Petróleos del Ecuador (PetroEcuador)*, ICSID Case No. ARB/08/5, Procedural Order No. 1 on Burlington Oriente's Request for Provisional Measures (June 29, 2009), para. 83.

123 *Burlington Resources Inc. and Others v. Republic of Ecuador and Empresa Estatal Petroleos del Ecuador*, ICSID Case No. ARB/08/5, Procedural Order No. 1 (June 29, 2009), para. 83.

124 *Perenco Ecuador Ltd. v. Republic of Ecuador and Empresa Estatal Petróleos del Ecuador (Petroecuador)*, ICSID Case No. ARB/08/6, Decision on Provisional Measures (May 8, 2009), para. 46.

125 See e.g. *Quiborax S.A., Non Metallic Minerals S.A. and Allan Fosk Kaplún v. Plurinational State of Bolivia*, ICSID Case No. ARB/06/2, Decision on Provisional Measures (Feb. 26, 2010), para. 122.

126 *Gerald International v. Sierra Leone*, ICSID Case No. ARB/19/31, Procedural Order No. 2: Decision on the Claimant's Request for Provisional Measures (July 28, 2020), para. 196.

127 *Italba Corporation v. Oriental Republic of* Uruquay, ICSID Case No. ARB/16/9, Decision on Claimant's Application for Provisional Measures and Temporary Relief (Feb. 15, 2017), para. 116.

coactively secure payment of the amounts allegedly owed by City Oriente pursuant to Law No. 2006–42, since this would entail a violation of the principle that neither party may aggravate or extend the dispute or take justice into their own hands."[128] It found that this was "precisely the case" because "the alleged crime—embezzlement—was precisely perpetrated through the non-payment of the amounts accrued on account of the application of the new Law."[129]

The specific factors that may give rise to a finding that the criminal proceedings have been conducted in bad faith are addressed in greater detail under the "proportionality" prong.

Second, the necessity of any interim relief will depend on the relief sought.

First, the most common type of relief sought has been **suspension of criminal proceedings** outright.

The record on this type of relief would appear to be mixed at first blush. The earlier decisions in *Quiborax* and *Lao Holding* ordered an outright suspension of ongoing criminal proceedings. In the 2016 *Hydro* decision, a tribunal ordered the suspension of ongoing criminal proceedings—only to walk that order back after the respondent State's extradition requests in one third country were rejected because. In the *Hydro* tribunal's words, this withdrawal was merited because "the principal objective for the Tribunal's recommendations has now been secured."[130] In the *Pugachev* case, by contrast, the tribunal found that, even with an international arrest warrant and extradition request, the claimant had "not provided conclusive evidence that shows that Claimant's ability to defend himself in the arbitration has been hindered by these proceedings."[131]

Yet, a detailed review of the case law reveals a more coherent approach. While, as the *Gerald International* tribunal explained, "[c]riminal investigations as such do not render the Claimant's right to freely present its case impossible,"[132] a number of factors have been found to compel a provisional measures order.

Access to Evidence: In *Quiborax*, the tribunal supported its decision with the finding that the "Claimants have been deprived of their corporate

---

128 *City Oriente Limited v. Republic of Ecuador*, ICSID Case No. ARB/06/21, Decision on Provisional Measures (Nov. 19, 2007), para. 62.

129 *City Oriente Limited v. Republic of Ecuador*, ICSID Case No. ARB/06/21, Decision on Provisional Measures (Nov. 19, 2007), para. 63.

130 *Hydro S.r.l. and others v. Republic of Albania*, ICSID Case No. ARB/15/28, Order on Provisional Measures (Mar. 3, 2016), para. 4.14.

131 *Sergei Viktorovich Pugachev v. Russia*, UNCITRAL, Interim Award (July 7, 2007), para. 280.

132 *Gerald International v. Sierra Leone*, ICSID Case No. ARB/19/31, Procedural Order No. 2: Decision on the Claimant's Request for Provisional Measures (July 28, 2020), para. 195.

records."[133] In *Nova*, by contrast, no documents had been confiscated and, in the tribunal's view, the claimant "has not explained why the Tribunal could not sufficiently address later, through evidentiary rulings any potential concerns about the use in this case of specific materials that allegedly were obtained through improper means."[134] The same conclusion was shared in the *Gerald International* case, in which the tribunal found that there was "no evidence at this time that the documents allegedly seized by police forces are in danger of being lost or destroyed or would otherwise not be available to the Claimant."[135]

Participation of a Party Representative or Key Witness: Participation of a party representative or key witness may also be a factor. In *Hydro*, for example, the tribunal found that the incarceration of two claimants and potential witnesses "would affect the ability of these two claimants and indeed other claimants to adequately put their cases and participate in the arbitration."[136] However, it bears noting that, where the threat of incarceration hangs over such individuals, more specific relief may be crafted and is often sought (as explained below).

Participation of Counsel: The *Teinver* tribunal (composed of Judge Thomas Buergenthal (chair), Henri Alvarez Q.C., and Kamal Hossain) confirmed that the threat of criminal proceedings against counsel in the arbitration "threatens to affect Claimants' right to be represented by counsel of their choice in this arbitration."[137] However, it did not issue any interim relief in part because, it explained, "it is not clear whether counsel or Claimants' court-appointed receivers are included within the scope of the investigation."[138] Likewise, in *Alicia Grace*, where criminal proceedings against counsel had been reported, but not confirmed, the Tribunal simply ordered the respondent State to confirm that no such proceedings were pending.[139]

---

133 *Quiborax S.A., Non Metallic Minerals S.A. and Allan Fosk Kaplún v. Plurinational State of Bolivia*, ICSID Case No. ARB/06/2, Decision on Provisional Measures (Feb. 26, 2010), para. 142.

134 *Nova Group Investments B.V. v. Romania*, ICSID Case No. ARB/16/19, Procedural Order No. 7, (Mar. 29, 2017), para. 335.

135 *Gerald International v. Sierra Leone*, ICSID Case No. ARB/19/31, Procedural Order No. 2: Decision on the Claimant's Request for Provisional Measures (July 28, 2020), para. 213.

136 *Hydro S.r.l. and others v. Republic of Albania*, ICSID Case No. ARB/15/28, Order on Provisional Measures (Mar. 3, 2016), para. 3.41.

137 *Teinver S.A., Transportes de Cercanias S.A. and Autobuses Urbanos del Sur S.A. v. Argentina*, ICSID Case No. ARB/09/1 (Apr. 8, 2016), para. 205.

138 *Teinver S.A., Transportes de Cercanias S.A. and Autobuses Urbanos del Sur S.A. v. Argentina*, ICSID Case No. ARB/09/1 (Apr. 8, 2016), para. 230.

139 *Alicia Grace and others v. United Mexican States*, ICSID Case No. UNCT/18/4, Procedural Order No. 6 (Dec. 19, 2019), para. 71.

Intimidation of Potential Witnesses and Others: In *Quiborax*, the tribunal noted that it was "troubled by the effect that criminal proceedings may have on potential witnesses."[140] Such effect—as the *Nova* tribunal made clear—must be demonstrated. While the *Quiborax* tribunal noted that "the very nature of these criminal proceedings is bound to reduce their willingness to cooperate in the ICSID proceeding,"[141] it pointed to a specific case where a potential witness was only released after he had confessed to the falsification of documents submitted in the arbitration.[142] The *Lao Holding* tribunal went even further, noting—without more—that a criminal proceeding (which was commenced as a result of an ongoing arbitration) would be a "powerful deterrent" to potential witnesses.[143] By contrast, however, the *Nova* tribunal declined to grant a broad order to suspend criminal proceedings, in part, because the claimant had not made out a case that such proceedings would discourage witnesses. In *Nova*, the issue appears to have been not one of principle (i.e. the *Nova* tribunal did not rule out that suspending criminal proceedings could be necessary to avoid a chilling effect on potential witnesses), but one of evidence. It found that only "specific allegations" would carry the claimant's evidentiary burden,[144] noting that "Nova has provided no information regarding who such witnesses are, why they are material to the integrity of this case, and why the Tribunal should accept that they are presently unwilling to testify because of the pending criminal proceedings."[145] In the *Ipek Investments* case, the tribunal was particularly concerned about both the bringing of criminal proceedings against family members as well as the indictment of lawyers to one of the relevant entities (although they do not appear to have been counsel in the arbitration).[146]

140 *Quiborax S.A., Non Metallic Minerals S.A. and Allan Fosk Kaplún v. Plurinational State of Bolivia*, ICSID Case No. ARB/06/2, Decision on Provisional Measures (Feb. 26, 2010), para. 143.

141 *Quiborax S.A., Non Metallic Minerals S.A. and Allan Fosk Kaplún v. Plurinational State of Bolivia*, ICSID Case No. ARB/06/2, Decision on Provisional Measures (Feb. 26, 2010), para. 146.

142 *Quiborax S.A., Non Metallic Minerals S.A. and Allan Fosk Kaplún v. Plurinational State of Bolivia*, ICSID Case No. ARB/06/2, Decision on Provisional Measures (Feb. 26, 2010), para. 145.

143 *Lao Holdings N.V. v. Lao People's Democratic Republic*, ICSID Case No. ARB(AF)/12/26, Ruling on Motion to Amend the Provisional Measures Order (May 30, 2014), para. 41.

144 *Nova Group Investments B.V. v. Romania*, ICSID Case No. ARB/16/19, Procedural Order No. 7 (Mar. 29, 2017), para. 333.

145 *Nova Group Investments B.V. v. Romania*, ICSID Case No. ARB/16/19, Procedural Order No. 7 (Mar. 29, 2017), para. 332.

146 *Ipek Investment Limited v. Republic of Turkey*, ICSID Case No. ARB/18/18, Procedural Order No. 5 (Sept. 19, 2019), para. 65.

By contrast, in *Convial Callao*, a tribunal declined to suspend criminal proceedings in respect of certain potential witnesses because it considered that the mere fact that criminal proceedings were pending would not impede those witnesses' participation in the arsbitration.[147] It did, however, order the respondent State to abstain from taking any action that would restrict those potential witnesses' freedom of movement.

Diversion of Resources: The mere existence of criminal proceedings, however, will generally not support a broad order just because those proceedings that would divert resources that could be committed to the arbitration. The *Nova* tribunal suggested that a claimant would need to show that such diversion would "cause those resources to become insufficient."[148]

Second, parties have sought **withdrawal of extradition requests**. No fewer than three different decisions have ordered withdrawal of extradition requests against claimant/party representatives who also were potential key witnesses:

- In *Hydro*, the tribunal's order that the respondent State withdraw an extradition request was based on a finding that the participation of claimants, party representatives, and potential witnesses was necessary.[149]
- In *Pugachev*, the tribunal found that a claimant's "ability to defend himself would be dramatically undermined" if extradited because his access to counsel and capacity to react promptly to developments would be limited.[150]
- The *Nova* tribunal's reasoning was twofold. First, it found that Mr. Adamescu could not continue to perform key functions **as party representative** while incarcerated. It stated: "Without reliable, confidential access to the inevitable and ongoing stream of email or telephone communications arising from a complex investor-state arbitration, or the ability to meet frequently in person on relatively short notice and for extended periods of time, it is difficult to see how functions effectively could be performed."[151] Second, in regards to Mr. Adamescu's presence **as a witness**, it noted that "Alexander Adamescu's availability as a witness is necessary for Nova to present its

147 *Convial Callao S.A. and CCI—Compañia de Concesiones de Infraestructura S.A. v. Peru*, Decisión sobre Solicitud de Medidas Provisionales, ICSID Case No. ARB/10/2 (Feb. 22, 2011), para. 124.

148 *Nova Group Investments B.V. v. Romania*, ICSID Case No. ARB/16/19, Procedural Order No. 7 (Mar. 29, 2017), para. 334.

149 *Hydro S.r.l. and others v. Republic of Albania*, ICSID Case No. ARB/15/28, Order on Provisional Measures (Mar. 3, 2016), para. 3.32.

150 *Sergei Viktorovich Pugachev v. Russia*, UNCITRAL, Interim Award (July 7, 2007), para. 319.

151 *Nova Group Investments B.V. v. Romania*, ICSID Case No. ARB/16/19, Procedural Order No. 7 (Mar. 29, 2017), para. 307.

case in any meaningful way."[152] According to the tribunal, participation via videoconference would not be enough given "the scope, length and importance of Mr. Adamescu's likely witness statements."[153] However, the *Nova* decision begs the question whether—in a post-COVID world—a tribunal would view an appearance via videoconference in the same light.

Third, parties have also sought the **release from custody** of relevant individuals. However, in contrast to the request for withdrawal of a pending extradition request that has not yet been executed, tribunals are reluctant to undo criminal law actions that have already been enforced.

This is the case even where the individual is key to the arbitration (e.g. a key witness or party representative). For example, in the Award on Emergency Measures in *Munshi v. Mongolia*, the sole arbitrator, Bernardo Cremades, did not order the release of the claimant, who was in a Mongolian prison, but only that the respondent State "to allow the Claimant to have reasonable access to both his local Mongolian counsel and to international counsel," without surveillance or interference and respecting the right to confidential communications with counsel.[154] Counsel had claimed that they had been unable to submit a witness statement from Mr. Munshi due to the conditions of his incarceration.[155] While the sole arbitrator noted that he was "deeply sympathetic" to arguments about the necessity of the claimant pursuing his claims from outside of prison, the sole arbitrator noted that he was "not satisfied that the Claimants (*sic*) fundamental rights in the procedural running of the arbitration extend so far as to interfere with the justice system of a sovereign state."[156] The sole arbitrator drew a distinction with other cases noting that, "[i]n the Claimant's case, he has already been convicted of a crime and sentenced to a term of imprisonment by Mongolian courts" and "[i]t is not for the Emergency Arbitrator to decide that the Claimant is in fact innocent."[157]

There would appear to be some tension here between this decision and those like the decision in the *Alicia Grace* case. That tribunal—comprised of

---

152 *Nova Group Investments B.V. v. Romania*, ICSID Case No. ARB/16/19, Procedural Order No. 7 (Mar. 29, 2017), para. 289.

153 *Nova Group Investments B.V. v. Romania*, ICSID Case No. ARB/16/19, Procedural Order No. 7 (Mar. 29, 2017), paras. 297–298.

154 *Mohammed Munshi v. Mongolia*, SCC EA 2018/007, Award on Emergency Measures (Feb. 5, 2018), para. 63.1.

155 *Mohammed Munshi v. Mongolia*, SCC EA 2018/007, Award on Emergency Measures (Feb. 5, 2018), footnote 2.

156 *Mohammed Munshi v. Mongolia*, SCC EA 2018/007, Award on Emergency Measures, February 5, 2018, para. 47.

157 *Mohammed Munshi v. Mongolia*, SCC EA 2018/007, Award on Emergency Measures (Feb. 5, 2018), para. 48.

Diego Fernández Arroyo (chair), Andrés Jana Linetzky, and Gabriel Bottini—rejected an order in relation to *future* arrest warrants, noting that "although the Tribunal is ready to accept that a possible detention of a Claimant and/or witness could affect and ultimately endanger Claimants' rights, at this stage such detention has not taken place, not being sufficient in the eyes of the Tribunal, the damage alleged by Claimants created by the possibility that such detention would occur."[158] It also declined to order any relief in relation to existing arrest warrants against claimants and relevant individuals because "it cannot be considered proven—at least so far—that the actions of the Mexican authorities are not based on regular procedures established in their criminal law."[159]

Moreover, in one case, a tribunal urged the respondent State to take steps to permit the protection of the investment—without interfering with the decision of that State's judiciary where the individuals are relevant to the investment. Here, of course, the only right that may be invoked is the right to non-aggravation. The *Gerald International* tribunal ordered a modification of bail conditions out of a concern for the security of the investment.[160] The employees had not been permitted by local authorities—but not the respondent State's judiciary (as in *Munshi*)—to return to the mine site at issue in the arbitration.[161]

Finally, in some cases, claimants have sought a **generic order** that the respondent State not take any measures to aggravate the dispute or carry out its arbitrations in good faith. While some tribunals have granted such relief,[162] others have declined on grounds that such obligations are already incumbent on both parties.[163] The *Gerald International* concluded that "such requests are too broad to permit the Tribunal to assess the risk of serious harm that could

158 *Alicia Grace and others v. United Mexican States*, ICSID Case No. UNCT/18/4, Procedural Order No. 6 (Dec. 19, 2019), para. 66.

159 *Alicia Grace and others v. United Mexican States*, ICSID Case No. UNCT/18/4, Procedural Order No. 6 (Dec. 19, 2019), para. 64.

160 *Gerald International v. Sierra Leone*, ICSID Case No. ARB/19/31, Procedural Order No. 2: Decision on the Claimant's Request for Provisional Measures (July 28, 2020), para. 209.

161 *Gerald International v. Sierra Leone*, ICSID Case No. ARB/19/31, Procedural Order No. 2: Decision on the Claimant s Request for Provisional Measures (July 28, 2020), para. 112.

162 *Caratube International Oil Company LLP & Devincci Salah Hourani v. Republic of Kazakhstan*, ICSID Case No. ARB/13/13, Decision on the Claimants' Request for Provisional Measures (Dec. 4, 2014), pp. 76–80.

163 *See e.g. Hydro S.r.l. and others v. Republic of Albania*, ICSID Case No. ARB/15/28, Order on Provisional Measures (Mar. 3, 2016), para. 4.4 ("The Tribunal decides that it is not appropriate to make any recommendation proposed in the terms sought by the Claimants in paragraph 4.1(d) above. In the first place, the measures sought are very broad, encompassing suspending or refraining from bringing 'any actions against the Claimants or their investments' and 'until the issuance of a Final Award'. Not only is this expressed in broad

materialize absent the Tribunal's order or to establish whether there is necessity and urgency for such an order in light of that risk."[164] By contrast, however, the *OOO Manolium Processing* tribunal (Juan Fernández-Armesto (chair), Stanimir Alexandrov, Brigitte Stern) *did* order such relief, affirming that "arbitral tribunals have consistently confirmed this duty, under which parties must abstain from any action which might aggravate or extend the dispute, alter the status quo, or take justice into their own hands."[165]

b *Urgency*

Urgency means that the provisional measure cannot await the rendering of the award.[166] Like necessity, the nature of urgency "will depend on the rights to be protected and the nature of the threat to those rights."[167] Two factors may influence a tribunal's assessment of urgency.

First, the right invoked by the party seeking interim measures may impact the tribunal's assessment of urgency.

Where relief is necessary to preserve procedural integrity, tribunals have found that "the requirement of urgency inherently is met"[168]—even where it is unclear that a criminal investigation will conclude before an award is rendered, as the *Teinver* tribunal found.[169]

---

terms, but it is premature because it is directed at actions not yet initiated and which may or may not be initiated at some time in the future").

164 *Gerald International v. Sierra Leone*, ICSID Case No. ARB/19/31, Procedural Order No. 2: Decision on the Claimant's Request for Provisional Measures (July 28, 2020), para. 220.

165 *OOO Manolium-Processing v. Belarus*, UNCITRAL, Decision on Claimant's Interim Measures Request (Dec. 1, 2018), para. 158.

166 *See* Christoph Schreuer, THE ICSID CONVENTION: A COMMENTARY: A COMMENTARY ON THE CONVENTION ON THE SETTLEMENT OF INVESTMENT DISPUTES BETWEEN STATES AND NATIONALS OF OTHER STATES (2009), p. 775; *Quiborax S.A., et. al. v. Plurinational State of Bolivia*, ICSID Case No. ARB/06/2, Decision on Provisional Measures (Feb. 26, 2010), para. 149; *Teinver S.A., Transportes de Cercanías S.A. and Autobuses Urbanos del Sur S.A. v. Argentine Republic*, ICSID Case No. ARB/09/1, Decision on Provisional Measures (Apr. 8, 2016), para. 233.

167 *See Nova Group Investments B.V. v. Romania*, ICSID Case No. ARB/16/19, Procedural Order No. 7 (Mar. 29, 2017), para. 241.

168 *Quiborax S.A., et. al. v. Plurinational State of Bolivia*, ICSID Case No. ARB/06/2, Decision on Provisional Measures (Feb. 26, 2010), para. 153; *Hydro S.r.l. and others v. Republic of Albania*, ICSID Case No. ARB/15/28, Order on Provisional Measures (Mar. 3, 2016), para. 3.29; *Nova Group Investments B.V. v. Romania*, ICSID Case No. ARB/16/19, Procedural Order No. 7 (Mar. 29, 2017), para. 241.

169 *Teinver S.A., Transportes de Cercanías S.A. and Autobuses Urbanos del Sur S.A. v. Argentine Republic*, ICSID Case No. ARB/09/1, Decision on Provisional Measures (Apr. 8, 2016), paras. 234–235.

Where the right is to the non-aggravation of the dispute, a tribunal need only establish that a party will suffer prejudice before the arbitral award is rendered.[170] However, it bears noting that the timing of the request for arbitration is largely irrelevant. ICSID tribunals "will assess urgency taking into account the entirety of the circumstances of the case"—in other words, notwithstanding the party's delayed submission.[171]

Second, the timing of the request for provisional measures may also have an impact on the urgency prong (of course, where the right invoked is a right to non-aggravation). In *Tokios Tokelés*, for example, the tribunal noted that the request could not be urgent given that the claimant had waited 18 months before seeking interim measures in relation to criminal proceedings:

> Moreover, the circumstances underlying the provisional measure requested do not appear urgent. Although the criminal proceedings against O.V. Danylov were initiated in March 2002—nine months before ICSID registered Claimant's Request for Arbitration Claimant did not include these proceedings in its first Request for Provisional Measures dated June 3, 2003, or its letter of June 24, 2003, to which Order No. 1 refers. Claimant cannot credibly claim that circumstances it did not consider urgent 18 months ago are urgent now.[172]

Timing may not only be relevant where the request is submitted a while after the conduct for which it seeks interim relief, but also where the conduct (and thus the request) comes late in the proceedings. In *Teinver*, the interim relief request was submitted late, just before the close of proceeding, by no fault of the claimants. Nonetheless, the tribunal found that there was no urgency as

170 *City Oriente Limited v. Republic of Ecuador*, ICSID Case No. ARB/06/21, Decision on Provisional Measures (Nov. 19, 2007), para. 69; *Burlington Resources Inc. and others v. Republic of Ecuador and Empresa Estatal Petróleos del Ecuador (PetroEcuador)*, ICSID Case No. ARB/08/5, Procedural Order No. 1 on Burlington Oriente's Request for Provisional Measures (June 29, 2009), para. 74.

171 *PNG Sustainable Development Program Ltd. V. Independent State of Papua New Guinea*, ICSID Case No. ARB/13/33 (Jan. 21, 2015), para. 117. *See also Hydro S.r.l. and others v. Republic of Albania*, ICSID Case No. ARB/15/28, Order on Provisional Measures (Mar. 3, 2016), para. 3.30 ("Whatever may be said about this delay, the Tribunal is in doubt that measures sought are now urgent").

172 *Tokios Tokelés v. Ukraine*, ICSID Case No. ARB/02/18, Procedural Order No. 3 (Jan. 18, 2005), para. 13.

the case was likely to conclude before any action would be taken against counsel for the claimants and others.[173]

However, timing may be less relevant where conduct is immminent, even though it has not occurred. Tribunals have moved to act before being presented with a *fait accompli*. In *Nova*, the tribunal sought to prevent extradition before that extradition had taken place because "it is far less clear how such a recommendation could be implemented *after* the English courts have ordered Mr. Adamescu's extradition, at which time that outcome becomes an edict of the English courts, and not simply a pending request from Romania."[174] This appears to be consistent with the *Munshi* tribunal's decision not to issue an order that a convicted claimant be released from prison.[175] However, it would appear to sit difficultly with the *Alicia Grace* tribunal's suggestion that the mere possibility of incarceration was not sufficient to merit an order for interim relief.[176] The difference, however, was that in *Alicia Grace*, the claimants sought broad relief (i.e. the suspension of pending criminal proceedings) and the result may have been different if the claimants had sought tailored relief in relation to specific potential witnesses.

c *Proportionality*

While not all tribunals have addressed proportionality as a separate prong of the test for interim measures,[177] they conduct some balancing assessment between the interests of the claimant and of the respondent State.

As a preliminary point, tribunals find that preliminary relief application in restraint of a State's criminal law measures must meet a "particularly high threshold," one stricter than where the measures whose restraint are sought do not relate to criminal proceeding.[178] Such a threshold is justified by the fact

173 *Teinver S.A., Transportes de Cercanias S.A. and Autobuses Urbanos del Sur S.A. v. Argentina*, ICSID Case No. ARB/09/1 (Apr. 8, 2016), para. 234.

174 *Nova Group Investments B.V. v. Romania*, ICSID Case No. ARB/16/19, Procedural Order No. 7 (Mar. 29, 2017), para. 312.

175 *Mohammed Munshi v. Mongolia*, SCC EA 2018/007, Award on Emergency Measures (Feb. 5, 2018), footnote 2.

176 *Alicia Grace and others v. United Mexican States*, ICSID Case No. UNCT/18/4, Procedural Order No. 6 (Dec. 19, 2019), para. 66.

177 *See e.g. Quiborax S.A., et. al. v. Plurinational State of Bolivia*, ICSID Case No. ARB/06/2, Decision on Provisional Measures (Feb. 26, 2010), Sections IV(C) and (D).

178 *Lao Holdings N.V. v. Lao People's Democratic Republic*, ICSID Case No. ARB(AF)/12/26, Ruling on Motion to Amend the Provisional Measures Order (May 30, 2014), para. 33; *Caratube International Oil Company LLP & Devincci Salah Hourani v. Republic of Kazakhstan*, ICSID Case No. ARB/13/13, Decision on the Claimants' Request for Provisional Measures (Dec. 4, 2014), para. 134 (noting that "criminal investigations and measures taken by a

that the interim measure would curtail activity that is a "right and duty" and "prerogative of any sovereign State"[179] and therefore such an interim measure is only justified in "exceptional circumstances"[180] where "special considerations" prevail.[181]

Of course (as we have seen), this does not mean that a tribunal may *never* order provisional measures restraining a State's exercise of its criminal law powers. Rather, it means that a tribunal will take special account for a State's sovereign "right and duty to conduct criminal prosecutions"[182] in its proportionality analysis.[183]

Under the proportionality requirement, an ICSID tribunal will require the interim relief requested to be sufficiently specific to protect the right that is threatened. In other words, the measures requested must constitute "minimum steps necessary to meet the objectives set out in the Convention."[184]

If a measure is overbroad, it may be rejected. In the *Hydro* case, for example, the tribunal declined to maintain an order that the host State suspend criminal proceedings, noting that the two relevant individuals were no longer subject to the threat of extradition and, therefore, there was "no need to order any provisional measures which would have the effect of impairing the

state in that context require special considerations"); *PNG Sustainable Development Program Ltd. V. Independent State of Papua New Guinea*, ICSID Case No. ARB/13/33 (Jan. 21, 2015), para. 145; *EuroGas Inc. And Belmont Resources Inc. v. Slovak Republic*, ICSID Case No. ARB/14/14, Procedural Order No. 3 (June 23, 2015), para. 77; *Teinver S.A., Transportes de Cercanías S.A. and Autobuses Urbanos del Sur S.A. v. Argentine Republic*, ICSID Case No. ARB/09/1, Decision on Provisional Measures (Apr. 8, 2016), para. 227; *Nova Group Investments B.V. v. Romania*, ICSID Case No. ARB/16/19, Procedural Order No. 7 (Mar. 29, 2017), para. 277; *Sergei Viktorovich Pugachev v. Russia*, UNCITRAL, Interim Award (July 7, 2007), paras. 214, 272.

179 *EuroGas Inc. And Belmont Resources Inc. v. Slovak Republic*, ICSID Case No. ARB/14/14, Procedural Order No. 3 (June 23, 2015), para. 77.

180 *EuroGas Inc. And Belmont Resources Inc. v. Slovak Republic*, ICSID Case No. ARB/14/14, Procedural Order No. 3 (June 23, 2015), para. 82.

181 *Caratube International Oil Company LLP & Devincci Salah Hourani v. Republic of Kazakhstan*, ICSID Case No. ARB/13/13, Decision on the Claimants' Request for Provisional Measures (Dec. 4, 2014), para. 134.

182 *EuroGas Inc. And Belmont Resources Inc. v. Slovak Republic*, ICSID Case No. ARB/14/14, Procedural Order No. 3 (June 23, 2015), para. 77.

183 While some tribunals have not expressly examined proportionality, they have given "serious consideration" to the effect of the provisional measures order on a State's sovereignty. *Quiborax S.A., et. al. v. Plurinational State of Bolivia*, ICSID Case No. ARB/06/2, Decision on Provisional Measures (Feb. 26, 2010), para. 164.

184 *Teinver S.A., Transportes de Cercanías S.A. and Autobuses Urbanos del Sur S.A. v. Argentine Republic*, ICSID Case No. ARB/09/1, Decision on Provisional Measures (Apr. 8, 2016), para. 227.

State's sovereign rights to exercise its police powers"[185] Similarly, in *Pugachev*, the tribunal found that a request for a bar to future criminal proceedings was "proportionate because it unduly and unjustifiably encroaches Russia's future ability to initiate criminal proceedings against any of the named individuals, and request international cooperation in this context, including extradition requests."[186] While the *Munshi* tribunal accepted that the claimant may have "legitimate issues" with a respondent State's judicial system, it did not believe that "it would be proportional, based on the evidence that has been submitted to the Emergency Arbitrator, to order Mongolia to relinquish its control of a person that has been tried and convicted of committing a crime under Mongolian law."[187]

However, where the measure is tailored narrowly to protect the right in jeopardy without infringing upon a State's sovereignty, it will be considered proportional to the harm caused to such sovereignty. For example, in *Nova Group* and *Hydro*, ICSID tribunals found that provisional measures preventing the extradition of key witnesses and party representatives was proportionate.[188] In the *Quiborax* case, the tribunal found that, where a State commenced a criminal investigation that, the tribunal found, was in retaliation for the arbitration, a "mere stay of the criminal proceedings would not affect Respondent's sovereignty nor require conduct in violation of national law" because "[o]nce this arbitration is finalized, Respondent will be free to continue the criminal proceedings"[189] (an approach echoed by the *Hydro* tribunal[190]). Where tribunals have ordered specific relief that does not affect the pendency of a criminal investigation or proceeding, they have noted the fact that an "[o]rder from this Tribunal will not affect the pendency of the criminal proceedings that have already been brought; nor will it preclude the continued pursuit of those proceedings against persons other than the Targeted Individuals," as the *Ipek* tribunal explained.[191]

---

185 *Hydro S.r.l. and others v. Republic of Albania*, ICSID Case No. ARB/15/28, Order on Provisional Measures (Mar. 3, 2016), para. 4.16.

186 *Sergei Viktorovich Pugachev v. Russia*, UNCITRAL, Interim Award (July 7, 2007), para. 300.

187 *Mohammed Munshi v. Mongolia*, SCC EA 2018/007, Award on Emergency Measures (Feb. 5, 2018), para. 56.

188 *PNG Sustainable Development Program Ltd. V. Independent State of Papua New Guinea*, ICSID Case No. ARB/13/33 (Jan. 21, 2015), para. 142.

189 *Quiborax S.A., et. al. v. Plurinational State of Bolivia*, ICSID Case No. ARB/06/2, Decision on Provisional Measures (Feb. 26, 2010), para. 165.

190 *Hydro S.r.l. and others v. Republic of Albania*, ICSID Case No. ARB/15/28, Order on Provisional Measures (Mar. 3, 2016), para. 3.41.

191 *Ipek Investment Limited v. Republic of Turkey*, ICSID Case No. ARB/18/18, Procedural Order No. 5 (Sept. 19, 2019), para. 69.

The *Quiborax* decision touches upon another potential element of the proportionality analysis: the good faith of the respondent State in commencing and pursuing the criminal proceedings. While the *Quiborax* tribunal found that the criminal proceedings in that case were commenced solely to develop a defense strategy in the arbitration,[192] it went so far as to note that **even if** there were a valid basis for a criminal prosecution, proportionality would weigh in favor of a the claimant where the "underlying motivation" of that proceeding was linked to the arbitration:

> Regardless of whether the criminal proceedings have a legitimate basis or not (an issue which the Tribunal is not in a position to determine), the direct relationship between the criminal proceedings and this ICSID arbitration is preventing Claimants from accessing witnesses that could be essential to their case.[193]

In other words, so long as the right whose protection is sought relates to the procedural integrity of the arbitration, the motivations behind the criminal measure against which relief is sought are irrelevant. Therefore, if criminal law measures prevent a claimant in any way from presenting its case, interim relief is merited.

In this vein, the *Lao Holding* tribunal echoed this finding, noting that it was "satisfied on the evidence that the primary purpose for which the Respondent intends to use the powers of criminal investigation, at least in the first instance, is to collect evidence for use at the arbitration, which, in the result, will undermine the integrity of the arbitral process."[194] In fact, the respondent State admitted that one of the objectives of its criminal proceeding was precisely "to enable it to develop evidence that will serve as part of its defence

---

192 *Quiborax S.A., et. al. v. Plurinational State of Bolivia*, ICSID Case No. ARB/06/2, Decision on Provisional Measures (Feb. 26, 2010), para. 122.

193 *Quiborax S.A., Non Metallic Minerals S.A. and Allan Fosk Kaplún v. Plurinational State of Bolivia*, ICSID Case No. ARB/06/2, Decision on Provisional Measures (Feb. 26, 2010), para. 163. See *id.*, para. 164 ("Although Bolivia may have reasons to suspect that the persons being prosecuted could have engaged in criminal conduct, the facts presented to the Tribunal suggest that the underlying motivation to initiate the criminal proceedings was their connection to this arbitration, which has been expressly deemed to constitute the harm caused to Bolivia that is required as one of the constituent elements of the crimes prosecuted").

194 *Lao Holdings N.V. v. Lao People's Democratic Republic*, ICSID Case No. ARB(AF)/12/26, Ruling on Motion to Amend the Provisional Measures Order (May 30, 2014), para. 26.

in the present arbitration proceedings."[195] But the *Lao Holding* tribunal went even further. It explained that "the integrity of the arbitral process would be compromised by permitting the Respondent to run a criminal investigation concurrently with the arbitration directed to the same people and the same facts at the same time."[196]

A number of more recent cases, however, have looked to the motivations behind the criminal proceedings without reference to whether the right whose protection is sought is one of procedural integrity or non-aggravation. For example, the *Gerald International* tribunal, noted that, while "seriously concerned about the temporal coincidence of the criminal investigations with the beginning of the present ICSID proceedings" and the "unclear connection" between various events and the arrests of claimant employees,[197] there was "no evidence at this time that the investigations were initiated in bad faith or by way of retaliation."[198] Likewise, the *Italba* tribunal rejected a request to suspend a criminal investigation because "there is no evidence on the record to support Claimant's contention that the criminal investigation in the present case has been brought in bad faith by the Uruguayan authorities."[199] While this would seem to create some tension with the *Quiborax* decision, such tension may only be superficial. In both *Gerald International* and *Italba*, the tribunals addressed a broad request for suspension of criminal proceedings, which do not in themselves affect a party's procedural rights.

These decisions beg the question whether the mere existence of concurrent criminal proceedings can lead to interim relief in relation to those proceedings—even where there is no evidence that those proceedings are being used to gain some advantage in the arbitration. That question has not yet been definitively answered by arbitral tribunals.

---

195 *Lao Holdings N.V. v. Lao People's Democratic Republic*, ICSID Case No. ARB(AF)/12/26, Ruling on Motion to Amend the Provisional Measures Order (May 30, 2014), para. 28.

196 *Lao Holdings N.V. v. Lao People's Democratic Republic*, ICSID Case No. ARB(AF)/12/26, Ruling on Motion to Amend the Provisional Measures Order (May 30, 2014), para. 39.

197 *Gerald International v. Sierra Leone*, ICSID Case No. ARB/19/31, Procedural Order No. 2: Decision on the Claimant's Request for Provisional Measures (July 28, 2020), para. 200.

198 *Gerald International v. Sierra Leone*, ICSID Case No. ARB/19/31, Procedural Order No. 2: Decision on the Claimant's Request for Provisional Measures (July 28, 2020), para. 202.

199 *Italba Corporation v. Oriental Republic of* Uruquay, ICSID Case No. ARB/16/9, Decision on Claimant's Application for Provisional Measures and Temporary Relief (Feb. 15, 2017), para. 116.

IV Effect

> I have no spur
> To prick the sides of my intent, but only
> Vaulting ambition, which o'erleaps itself
> And falls on the other.
>
> W. SHAKESPEARE, Macbeth, *lns. 498–501*

Unlike a State court, an investor-State tribunal has no authority to ensure compliance with its procedural orders (except, of course, its "vaulting ambition" that such orders be complied with). Moreover, once an order is rendered, questions may be raised about the binding effect of interim relief (**a**) and the duration of such effect (including, a respondent State's ability to seek reconsideration of the order) (**b**).

a *The Binding Effect of Interim Relief*

Regardless of its form (procedural order, interim award, decision of an emergency arbitrator, or other), interim relief must be binding for its compliance to have any meaning.

Under most arbitral rules, there is little question that interim relief binds the party against whom such relief has been ordered. For example, under the 1976 UNCITRAL Rules, for example, "the arbitral tribunal may take any interim measures it deems necessary in respect of the subject-matter of the dispute," including in the form of an interim award.[200] Likewise, the 2021 ICC Rules provide that "the arbitral tribunal may, at the request of a party, order any interim or conservatory measure it deems appropriate."[201]

By contrast, Article 47 of the ICSID Convention provides that a tribunal may "recommend" interim relief. Here, it choses language similar to the ICJ Statute's Article 41, which provides that a tribunal may "indicate" such relief. The ICSID drafting history reveals that, while initial drafts included the more imperative "prescribe," this term was replaced by "recommend" after the Chinese delegate "felt the word 'prescribe' was too strong and was not necessary, since if there was any damage it could be included in the final award."[202] That justification of

200 Arbitration Rules (United Nations Commission on International Trade Law [UNCITRAL]) [1976], UN Doc A/31/98, 31st Session Supp No 17, Article 26(1).

201 Arbitration Rules (International Chamber of Commerce [ICC]) [2021] [available at https://iccwbo.org/content/uploads/sites/3/2020/12/icc-2021-arbitration-rules-2014-mediation-rules-english-version.pdf], Article 28(1).

202 History of the ICSID Convention: Volume II [available at https://icsid.worldbank.org/resources/publications/the-history-of-the-icsid-convention], p. 813.

the Chinese delegate, of course, does not exclude the binding force of interim relief. After all, interim relief must be mandatory if damage caused by non-compliance is to be compensated in the final award.

Since then, ICSID tribunals have been all but unanimous in finding that interim relief is mandatory until the award is rendered or the tribunal exercises its power to modify or revoke its interim relief decision.[203]

Here, they have again followed the cue of the ICJ. In its decision in the *LaGrand* case, the ICJ found that, notwithstanding the language of Article 41, the interim relief ordered was mandatory because "[i]t follows from the object and purpose of the Statute, as well as from the terms of Article 41 when read in their context, that the power to indicate provisional measures entails that such measures should be binding, inasmuch as the power in question is based on the necessity, when the circumstances call for it, to safeguard, and to avoid prejudice to, the rights of the parties as determined by the final judgment of the Court."[204] Subsequent decisions of the ICJ have made no mention of Article 41, but instead refer to "inherent powers of jurisdiction."[205]

This logic has been adopted by ICSID tribunals. Thus, for example, in *Pey Casado v. Chile*, the tribunal found that the ICJ's logic "appears manifestly applicable by analogy to article 47 of the ICSID Convention."[206]

At least two tribunals have offered a different basis for the binding effect of interim relief in the ICSID system. In *Maffezini v. Spain*, a case that predated the *LaGrand* decision, the tribunal found that provisional measures were mandatory under the ICSID Convention because Rule 39 of the ICSID Arbitration Rules in their Spanish version refers to an order as a "dictación."[207] According to the tribunal, the "parties to the Convention [*did not mean*] to create a

203 *See e.g. Emilio Agustín Maffezini v. Kingdom v. Spain*, ICSID Case No. ARB/97/7, Procedural Order No. 2 (Oct. 28, 1999), para. 9; *Víctor Pey Casado & Fondation Président Allende v. Republic of Chile*, ICSID Case No. ICSID/ARB/98/2, Décision sur les Mesures Conservatoires sollicités par les Parties (Sept. 25, 2001). *But see Caratube International Oil Company LLP v. Republic of Kazakhstan*, ICSID Case No. ARB/08/12, Decision Regarding Claimant's Application for Provisional Measures (July 31, 2009), para. 67.

204 *LaGrand (Germany v United States)*, [1999] ICJ Rep 466 (Mar. 3, 1999), 503.

205 *Northern Cameroons, (Cameroon v United Kingdom)*, Preliminary Objections, Separate Opinion of Judge Gerald Fitzmaurice, [1963] ICJ Rep 15, ICGJ 153 (ICJ 1963) (Dec. 2, 1963), 107. See also *Nuclear Tests (Australia v. France)*, Preliminary Objections, Order, [1973] ICJ Rep. 97 (June 22, 1973), 109; *Nuclear Tests (New Zealand v. France)*, [1973] ICJ Rep. 135 (June 22, 1975), 145.

206 *Víctor Pey Casado & Fondation Président Allende v. Republic of Chile*, ICSID Case No. ICSID/ARB/98/2, Décision sur les Mesures Conservatoires sollicités par les Parties (Sept. 25, 2001), para. 20.

207 *Emilio Agustín Maffezini v. Kingdom v. Spain*, ICSID Case No. ARB/97/7, Procedural Order No. 2, (Oct. 28, 1999), para. 9.

substantial difference in the effect of these two words" (i.e. "recommend" and "dictación"[208]). This approach was also taken by the *City Oriente* tribunal.[209]

However, the *City Oriente* tribunal explained that such power is inherent as it results from the purpose of Article 47 (to provide effective judicial protection of a party's rights) and the express requirement in the provision that any interim measure be necessary:

> Even disregarding such semantic discussion, a teleological interpretation of both provisions leads to the conclusion that the provisional measures recommended are necessarily binding. The Tribunal may only order such measures if their adoption is necessary to preserve the rights of the parties and guarantee that the award will fulfill its purpose of providing effective judicial protection. Such goals may only be reached if the measures are binding, and they share the exact same binding nature as the final arbitral award. Therefore, it is the Tribunal's conclusion that the word "recommend" is equal in value to the word "order."[210]

This approach makes sense—particularly, in light of (i) the fact that Article 44 allows a tribunal to decide where "any question of procedure arises which is not covered"[211] and (ii) other tribunals, like the *Teinver* tribunal, based their finding that an order is binding on "the inherent jurisdiction and powers required to preserve the integrity of its own process and the duty to ensure that the Parties comply with their obligation to arbitrate fairly."[212]

---

208 *Emilio Agustín Maffezini v. Kingdom v. Spain*, ICSID Case No. ARB/97/7, Procedural Order No. 2 (Oct. 28, 1999), para. 9.

209 *City Oriente Limited v. Republic of Ecuador and Empresa Estatal Petróleos del Ecuador (Petroecuador)* [*I*], ICSID Case No. ARB/06/21, Decision on Provisional Measures (Nov. 19, 2007), para. 52.

210 *City Oriente Limited v. Republic of Ecuador and Empresa Estatal Petróleos del Ecuador (Petroecuador)* [*I*], ICSID Case No. ARB/06/21, Decision on Provisional Measures (Nov. 19, 2007), para. 52.

211 Convention on the Settlement of Investment Disputes Between States and Nationals of Other States (International Centre for Settlement of Investment Disputes [ICSID]) 575 UNTS 159 (1966).

212 *Teinver S.A., Transportes de Cercanías S.A. and Autobuses Urbanos del Sur S.A. v. Argentine Republic*, ICSID Case No. ARB/09/1, Decision on Provisional Measures (Apr. 8, 2016), para. 186. *See also Libananco Holdings Co. Ltd. v. Turkey*, ICSID Case No. ARB/06/8, Decision on Preliminary Issues (June 23, 2008), para. 78.

b *The Respondent State's Recourse against an Interim Measures Order*

The interim relief granted by the tribunal will last until an award is rendered or until the tribunal modifies or revokes that relief. Concurrent with the power to order interim relief is the power to revoke or modify interim relief that has been ordered. Such a power is expressly provided under ICSID Arbitration Rule 39(3), which states that a tribunal may "at any time modify or revoke its recommendations."[213] Therefore, a respondent State that is unhappy with the interim relief ordered against it is armed with a powerful tool.

However, to make use of this tool, it must show "changed circumstances." In *Hydro*, for example, the tribunal found that the decision of a UK court to stay *sine die* extradition proceedings was such a circumstance because the two claimants targeted by the respondent State's extradition request were "fully able to participate in the arbitration."[214] As such, in the *Hydro* tribunal's view, there was "no need to order any provisional measures which would have the effect of impairing the State's sovereign rights to exercise its police powers."[215] The *Nova* tribunal, by contrast, declined to revoke or modify its order because "Romania does not suggest that any circumstances have changed in the short time since the Tribunal's issuance of the Decision."[216]

The power to seek revocation or modification, therefore, is not an absolute one, but must obey the logic of the original decision.

V The Consequences of Non-Compliance

> Can'st thou, O partial sleep! give thy repose
> To the wet sea-boy in an hour so rude;
> And, in the calmest and most stillest night,
> With all appliances and means to boot,

213 ARBITRATION RULES (INTERNATIONAL CENTRE FOR SETTLEMENT OF INVESTMENT DISPUTES [ICSID]) [available at https://icsid.worldbank.org/sites/default/files/ICSID%20Convention%20English.pdf], Rule 39(3).

214 *Hydro S.r.l. and others v. Republic of Albania*, ICSID Case No. ARB/15/28, Decision on Claimants' Request for a Partial Award and Respondent's Application for Revocation or Modification of the Order on Provisional Measures (Sept. 1, 2016), para. 4.16.

215 *Hydro S.r.l. and others v. Republic of Albania*, ICSID Case No. ARB/15/28, Decision on Claimants' Request for a Partial Award and Respondent's Application for Revocation or Modification of the Order on Provisional Measures (Sept. 1, 2016), para. 4.16.

216 *Nova Group Investments B.V. v. Romania*, ICSID Case No. ARB/16/19, Procedural Order No. 8 Concerning Respondent's Request for Reconsideration of Procedural Order No. 7 (Apr. 18, 2017), para. 32.

> Deny it to a king? Then, happy low, lie down!
> 'Uneasy lies the head that wears a crown'.
>
> W. SHAKESPEARE, Henry IV, *lns. 1730–1735*

What is a claimant to do when a respondent State refuses to comply with interim relief that has been granted by an investor-State tribunal? While it has been suggested that a tribunal may account for any damage in its final award, that will be of little solace to a claimant whose ability to pursue the arbitration has been hindered by conduct unrelated to its claim on the merits. After all, the claimant's right to procedural integrity (if, for example, a claimant is fully prevented from pursuing its claim) cannot be compensated with monetary relief. Instead, a claimant may be able to seek assistance from State courts (**a**) or the tribunal itself (**b**).

a *Enforcement before a State Court*

Neither the ICSID Convention nor any relevant arbitral regime provides expressly for the enforceability of interim relief before State courts—no matter the form of the instrument in which that relief is ordered, i.e. a procedural order, interim award, or award of an energy arbitrator.

At least as far as the ICSID regime is concerned, this reality appears to be the result of a misapprehension of the full nature of interim relief. As the ICSID Convention's drafting history reveals, while it was suggested that interim relief should take the form of an interim award, which "should be enforceable on the same basis as a final award," that proposal was rebuffed. The reason: interim relief may be revoked at any time and, as such, "should not and need not be enforceable on the same basis as final awards" and, in any event, "the government may be held, in the final award for the investor, liable to pay damages for failure to conform to recommendations of provisional measures."[217] That approach, however, fails to take into account the special nature of prejudice to the right to procedural integrity, as we have seen.

Yet, all is not lost for a claimant against a non-compliant respondent State. The interim relief order is still a binding order rendered pursuant to a State's international law obligations.

In the respondent State, a claimant may be able to take advantage of mandatory provisions establishing the superiority of international law over domestic

217 HISTORY OF THE ICSID CONVENTION: VOLUME II [available at https://icsid.worldbank.org/resources/publications/the-history-of-the-icsid-convention] (1971), p. 655.

law.[218] As a practical matter, however, the claimant may find limited success before the local courts of the host State.

Where the relevant proceedings take place outside of the respondent State, chances of success may be greater. In *Hydro*, for example, a UK Magistrate Judge found that she could not "continue with the proceedings at this stage given the [*Hydro tribunal's provisional measures order*] is binding on the Government" of Albania and Albania "would be in breach of an international law obligation,"[219] although her principle finding was that a stay *sine die* was merited because Albania had misrepresented its own law and thus committed an abuse of process.[220] Yet, any hope that an investor-State order could be immediately enforceable in UK extradition proceedings is tempered by the decision of another UK Magistrate Judge in the *Nova* case. There, the judge declined to refuse an extradition request, reasoning that an order made pursuant to the ICSID Convention was "not binding on this court."[221] Extradition was upheld on appeal before the High Court, although the binding force of the provisional measures order does not seem to have been raised.[222]

If the experience before UK courts is any judge, at best, the interim order may be considered by State courts as nothing more than a factor in its ultimate decision.

---

218 *See e.g. Murray v. The Schooner Charming Betsy*, 6 U.S. 64 (U.S. 1804) (finding that national statutes should be interpreted in such a way that the interpretation does not conflict with international laws); Grundgesetz [GG] [Basic Law] [English translation available at http://www.gesetze-im-internet.de/englisch_gg/index.html], Article 25 ("The general rules of international law shall be an integral part of federal law. They shall take precedence over the laws and directly create rights and duties for the inhabitants of the federal territory.").

219 *Government of Albania v. Francesco Becchetti and Mauro De Renzis*, Decision of the Westminster Magistrates' Court (May 20, 2016), [available at https://www.italaw.com/sites/default/files/case-documents/italaw7644.pdf] (last visited on Apr. 7, 2021), para. 54.

220 See *Government of Albania v. Francesco Becchetti and Mauro De Renzis*, Decision of the Westminster Magistrates' Court (May 20, 2016), [available at https://www.italaw.com/sites/default/files/case-documents/italaw7644.pdf] (last visited on Apr. 7, 2021), para. 53. The Court, however, wrongly suggested that the provisional measures order in question was "binding on this court."

221 *Bucharest Appeal Court v. Bogdan-Alexander Adamescu*, Decision of the Westminster Magistrates' Court (Aug. 23, 2017) [available at https://www.italaw.com/sites/default/files/case-documents/italaw10489.pdf] (last visited on Apr. 7, 2021), para. 94.

222 *Bucharest Appeal Court v. Bogdan-Alexander Adamescu*, Decision of the Westminster Magistrates' Court (Aug. 23, 2017) [available at https://www.italaw.com/sites/default/files/case-documents/italaw10489.pdf] (last visited on Apr. 7, 2021), (Aug. 23, 2017).

b *Enforcement before an Arbitral Tribunal*

Another enforcement option may exist: enforcement before the arbitral tribunal. The tools in the tribunal's chest are limited, but one merits further consideration: the tribunal's authority to impose a penalty for non-compliance.

Such an option was expressly debated in the drafting history of the ICSID Convention, but any express reference to such authority was ruled out as, it was considered, any damage could be taken into account in the final award.[223] That, as we have noted, is insufficient where the prejudice is to the procedural integrity of the arbitration, which is entirely unrelated to the merits. Yes, a claimant could potentially bring claims for treaty breach based on the respondent State's non-compliance, but such a claim may only be theoretical in nature if the consequences of the respondent State's breach are grievous. Moreover, at least one tribunal (the *Quiborax* tribunal) declined to find that a State's failure to arbitrate in good faith was a breach of its international obligations—although its finding appears to be factual, not legal ("while the criminal proceedings have undoubtedly increased the climate of hostility in which this arbitration unfolded, they have not rendered the solution to the dispute more difficult").[224] Another suggestion—that the tribunal draw adverse inferences on the basis of the State's conduct—is not likely to be of any assistance. The criminal proceedings may not go to the merits. Even if the criminal proceedings *do* relate to the merits, where they do not directly affect the investment, there may be no direct effect on valuation or damages. For example, if a State's actions prevent the claimant from presenting key factual or witness evidence or hinder access to a party representative, a simple costs award may be insufficient.

Article 44 of the ICSID Convention, however, may offer some relief to a prejudiced claimant. In relevant part, it provides:

> If any question of procedure arises which is not covered by this Section or the Arbitration Rules or any rules agreed by the parties, the Tribunal shall decide the question.[225]

---

223 History of the ICSID Convention: Volume II [available at https://icsid.worldbank.org/resources/publications/the-history-of-the-icsid-convention] (1971), p. 813.

224 *Quiborax S.A., Non Metallic Minerals S.A. and Allan Fosk Kaplún v. Plurinational State of Bolivia*, ICSID Case No. ARB/06/2, Award (Sept. 16, 2015), para. 594.

225 Convention on the Settlement of Investment Disputes Between States and Nationals of Other States (International Centre for Settlement of Investment Disputes [ICSID]) 575 UNTS 159 (1966).

Article 44 has been invoked in one case already to sanction a party's failure to comply with an ICSID order. In *RSM v. Santa Lucia*, an ICSID tribunal that had issued a provisional measures order—albeit one for security for costs, not in relation to criminal law measures—ordered discontinuance of arbitral proceedings following the claimant's failure to comply with the order.[226] The tribunal found that Article 44(2) of the ICSID Convention allowed it to sanction non-compliance with discontinuance because an adverse inference would not provide any relief to the claimants.

The only tribunal to have considered the issue—the *Hydro* tribunal—declined to impose a penalty, but did not close the door. It stated that it was "not persuaded that the conduct of Respondent was such as to involve a contravention of the recommendation."[227] However, it did suggest that, where monetary compensation awarded in the final award would adequately compensate for any loss caused by non-compliance, a penalty would not be appropriate.[228] Taking the *Hydro* tribunal's reasoning *a contrario*, under the right circumstances, a tribunal (according to the *Hydro* tribunal) may order a penalty—for example, a daily penalty for each day of non-compliance or simply an award of legal or other costs incurred payable in the final award.

In non-ICSID arbitrations, the option may be an even more attractive one. Domestic arbitral laws also permit arbitral tribunals to order a penalty for non-compliance with its orders. For example, Article 1468 of the French Civil Code provides that "the arbitral tribunal may order the parties, pursuant to the conditions he or she determines **and under penalty for non-compliance**, any conservatory or provisional measure that he judges opportune."[229] Such

226 *RSM Production Corporation v. Santa Lucia*, ICSID Case No. ARB/12/10, Decision on Saint Lucia's Request for Suspension or Discontinuation of Proceedings (Apr. 8, 2015). While that award was annulled on grounds that the tribunal discontinuation of the proceedings with prejudice was effectively a dismissal of the case on the merits was an excess of power. That, of course, does not apply to the imposition of penalty. Indeed, the *RSM* annulment committee expressly decided that discontinuation of the proceedings was a procedural matter that would not exceed the powers of the tribunal. *RSM Production Corporation v. Santa Lucia*, ICSID Case No. ARB/12/10, Decision on Annulment (Apr. 29, 2019).

227 *Hydro S.r.l. and others v. Republic of Albania*, ICSID Case No. ARB/15/28, Decision on Claimants' Request for a Partial Award and Respondent's Application for Revocation or Modification of the Order on Provisional Measures (Sept. 1, 2016), para. 4.30.

228 *Hydro S.r.l. and others v. Republic of Albania*, ICSID Case No. ARB/15/28, Decision on Claimants' Request for a Partial Award and Respondent's Application for Revocation or Modification of the Order on Provisional Measures (Sept. 1, 2016), para. 4.30.

229 French C.P.C., Article 1468 [available at https://www.legifrance.gouv.fr/codes/section_lc/LEGITEXT000006070716/LEGISCTA000006089134/#LEGISCTA000006089134] (author's translation).

authority may also exist even where no express authority is granted to the arbitrator by the law of the seat.[230]

Even where such provisions do exist, however, questions abound. A tribunal must establish (i) what conditions may apply to any such relief and (ii) how much any penalty should be. Naturally, a penalty is a form of interim relief and the same conditions (necessity, urgency, proportionality) should apply, but should they be applied in the same way? In other words, does every interim measure necessarily give rise to a right to a penalty for non-compliance? Likewise, how much of a penalty is enough? Does the penalty amount depend on the financial means of the respondent State or, for example, the respondent State's determination to flout its obligations under the interim relief?

Where such a penalty is sought, the tribunal's task is an unenviable one (particularly given that prior decisions are of little (if any) assistance). Does it allow its *imperium* to be cast asunder by a State's brazen violation of the claimant's rights? Or does it charge ahead and deliver the respondent State a hefty bill whose bottom line has no relation to actual damages suffered by the claimant—simply to restrict conduct that falls squarely within a State's sovereign prerogative? Uneasy, indeed, lies the head that wears a crown.

References

18 CFR § 385.1113.

2019 Empirical Study: Provisional Measures in Investor-State Arbitration [available at https://www.biicl.org/publications/2019-empirical-study-provisional-measures-in-investorstate-arbitration] (last visited on Apr. 7, 2021).

Abaclat v. Republic of Argentina, ICSID Case No. ARB/07/5, Procedural Order No. 13 (Sept. 27, 2012).

Aegean Sea Continental Shelf (*Greece v. Turkey*), [1976] ICJ Rep 3 (Separate Opinion of President Jimenez de Arechaga).

Alicia Grace and others v. United Mexican States, ICSID Case No. UNCT/18/4, Procedural Order No. 6 (Dec. 19, 2019).

Allendale Mut. Ins. Co. v. Bull Data Sys., Inc., 10 F.3d 425, 431 (7th Cir. 1993).

Application of the International Convention on the Elimination of All Forms of Racial Discrimination (*Qatar v. United Arab Emirates*) [2018] ICJ Rep. 406 (Jul. 23, 2018).

230 *See e.g.* A. Mourre "Chapter 2: Judicial Penalties and Specific Performance in International Arbitration" in INTEREST, AUXILIARY AND ALTERNATIVE REMEDIES IN INTERNATIONAL ARBITRATION (Kluwer, 2008).

ARBITRATION RULES (INTERNATIONAL CENTRE FOR SETTLEMENT OF INVESTMENT DISPUTES [ICSID]) [available at https://icsid.worldbank.org/sites/default/files/ICSID%20Convention%20English.pdf] (last visited on Apr. 7, 2021).

ARBITRATION RULES (INTERNATIONAL CHAMBER OF COMMERCE [ICC]) [2021] [available at https://iccwbo.org/content/uploads/sites/3/2020/12/icc-2021-arbitration-rules-2014-mediation-rules-english-version.pdf] (last visited on Apr. 7, 2021).

Arbitration Rules (United Nations Commission on International Trade Law [UNCITRAL]) [1976] UN Doc A/31/98, 31st Session Supp No 17.

Avena and Other Mexican Nationals (*Mexico v United States*), [2003] ICJ Rep. 77 (Feb. 5, 2003).

Avena and Other Mexican Nationals (*Mexico v United States*), [2003] ICJ Rep. 77 (Feb. 5, 2003); *Jadhav Case* (*India v. Pakistan*) [2017] ICJ Rep. 231 (May 18, 2017).

Biwater Gauff (Tanzania) Ltd. v. United Republic of Tanzania, ICSID Case No. ARB/05/22, Procedural Order No. 3 (Sept. 29, 2006).

Born, G. International Commercial Arbitration (3rd ed., Kluwer, 2020).

Bucharest Appeal Court v. Bogdan-Alexander Adamescu, Decision of the Westminster Magistrates' Court (Aug. 23, 2017) [availablae at https://www.italaw.com/sites/default/files/case-documents/italaw10489.pdf] (last visited on Apr. 7, 2021).

Burlington Resources Inc. and Others v. Republic of Ecuador and Empresa Estatal Petroleos del Ecuador, ICSID Case No. ARB/08/5, Procedural Order No. 1 (June 29, 2009).

Caratube International Oil Company LLP and Devincci Salah Hourani v. Republic of Kazakhstan, ICSID Case No. ARB/13/13, Decision on the Claimant's Request for Provisional Measures (Dec. 4, 2014).

Caratube International Oil Company LLP v. Republic of Kazakhstan, ICSID Case No. ARB/08/12, Decision Regarding Claimant's Application for Provisional Measures, (July 31, 2009).

Case of Certain Criminal Proceedings in France (*France v. Congo*), [2003] I.C.J. Rep., 102 (Jun. 17, 2003).

Certain Activities carried out by Nicaragua in the Border Area; Construction of a Road in Costa Rica along the San Juan River (*Costa Rica v Nicaragua*), [2013].

Ceskoslovenska Obchodni Banka, A.S. v. The Slovak Republic, ICSID Case No. ARB/97/4, Procedural Order No. 2 (Sept. 9, 1998).

Churchill Mining PLC v. Republic of Indonesia, ICSID Case No. ARB/12/14, Procedural Order No. 3 (March 4, 2013).

City Oriente Limited v. Republic of Ecuador and Empresa Estatal Petróleos del Ecuador (Petroecuador) [*I*], ICSID Case No. ARB/06/21, Decision on Provisional Measures (Nov. 19, 2007).

Collins, L. "*Provisional and Protective Measures in International Litigation*," in RECUEIL DES COURS, COLLECTED COURSES OF THE HAGUE ACADEMY OF INTERNATIONAL LAW, Vol. 234 (1992).

Compare Salini et al v. Morocco, ICSID Case No. ARB/00/4, Decision on Jurisdiction (July 23, 2001).

CONVENTION ON THE SETTLEMENT OF INVESTMENT DISPUTES BETWEEN STATES AND NATIONALS OF OTHER STATES (International Centre for Settlement of Investment Disputes [ICSID]) 575 UNTS 159 (1966).

Convial Callao S.A. and CCI—Compañia de Concesiones de Infraestructura S.A. v. Peru, Decisión sobre Solicitud de Medidas Provisionales, ICSID Case No. ARB/10/2 (Feb. 22, 2011).

Douglas, Z. The International Law of Investment Claims (Cambridge University Press, 2010).

Emilio Agustín Maffezini v. Kingdom v. Spain, ICSID Case No. ARB/97/7, Procedural Order No. 2 (Oct. 28, 1999).

EuroGas Inc. And Belmont Resources Inc. v. Slovak Republic, ICSID Case No. ARB/14/14, Procedural Order No. 3 (June 23, 2015).

French Code of Civil Procedure, Article 484 [available at https://www.legifrance.gouv.fr/codes/section_lc/LEGITEXT000006070716/LEGISCTA000006089134/#LEGISCTA000006089134] (last visited on Apr. 7, 2021).

Gerald International v. Sierra Leone, ICSID Case No. ARB/19/31, Procedural Order No. 2: Decision on the Claimant's Request for Provisional Measures (July 28, 2020).

Government of Albania v. Francesco Becchetti and Mauro De Renzis, Decision of the Westminster Magistrates' Court (May 20, 2016), [available at https://www.italaw.com/sites/default/files/case-documents/italaw7644.pdf] (last visited on Apr. 7, 2021).

Grundgesetz [GG] [Basic Law] [English translation available at http://www.gesetze-im-internet.de/englisch_gg/index.html] (last visited on Apr. 7, 2021).

HISTORY OF THE ICSID CONVENTION: VOLUME II (1970) [available at https://icsid.worldbank.org/resources/publications/the-history-of-the-icsid-convention] (last visited on Apr. 7, 2021).

Hydro S.r.l. and others v. Republic of Albania, ICSID Case No. ARB/15/28, Order on Provisional Measures (Mar. 3, 2016).

Hydro S.r.l. and others v. Republic of Albania, ICSID Case No. ARB/15/28, Decision on Claimants' Request for a Partial Award and Respondent's Application for Revocation or Modification of the Order on Provisional Measures (Sept. 1, 2016).

Ipek Investment Limited v. Republic of Turkey, ICSID Case No. ARB/18/18, Procedural Order No. 5 (Sept. 19, 2019).

Italba Corporation v. Oriental Republic of Uruguay, ICSID Case No. ARB/16/9, Decision on Claimant's Application for Provisional Measures and Temporary Relief (Feb. 15, 2017).

LaGrand (Germany v United States), [1999] ICJ Rep. 9 (Mar. 3, 1999).

Lao Holdings N.V. v. Lao People's Democratic Republic, ICSID Case No. ARB(AF)/12/26, Ruling on Motion to Amend the Provisional Measures Order (May 30, 2014).

League of Nations, STATUTE OF THE PERMANENT COURT OF INTERNATIONAL JUSTICE (Dec. 16, 1920).

Lenovo (United States) Inc. and others v. IPCom GmbH & Co. Kg, French Court of Appeal, No. 14/2020 (Mar. 3, 2015).

Libananco Holding Co. Ltd. V. Turkey, ICSID Case No. ARB/06/8, Preliminary Decision (June 23, 2008).

Mareva Compania Naviera SA v. International Bulkcarriers SA, [1975] 2 Lloyd's Rep 509 (C.A. June 23, 1975), [1980] 1 All ER 21.

Maria Lazareva v. Kuwait, UNCITRAL, Claimant's Application for Interim Measures under Article 26(1) (Mar. 27, 2019).

Michaels, R. "*Recognition and Enforcement of Foreign Judgments*," MAX PLANCK ENCYCLOPEDIA OF PUBLIC INTERNATIONAL LAW (2009).

Microsoft Corp. v. Motorola, Inc., 696 F.3d 872, 886 (9th Cir. 2012).

Miles, C. PROVISIONAL MEASURES BEFORE INTERNATIONAL COURTS AND TRIBUNALS (Cambridge University Press, 2017), Chapter 2: Origins of Provisional Matters.

Millicom International Operations B.V. and Sentel GSM SA v. Republic of Senegal, Decision on the Application for Provisional Measures (Aug. 24, 2009).

Mohammed Munshi v. Mongolia, SCC EA 2018/007, Award on Emergency Measures (Feb. 5, 2018).

Mourre, A. "*Chapter 2: Judicial Penalties and Specific Performance in International Arbitration*" in INTEREST, AUXILIARY AND ALTERNATIVE REMEDIES IN INTERNATIONAL ARBITRATION (Kluwer, 2008).

Murray v. The Schooner Charming Betsy, 6 U.S. 64 (U.S. 1804).

Northern Cameroons, (Cameroon v United Kingdom), Preliminary Objections, Separate Opinion of Judge Gerald Fitzmaurice, [1963] ICJ Rep 15, ICGJ 153 (ICJ 1963) (Dec. 2, 1963).

Nova Group Investments B.V. v. Romania, ICSID Case No. ARB/16/19, Procedural Order No. 7 (Mar. 29, 2017).

Nova Group Investments B.V. v. Romania, ICSID Case No. ARB/16/19, Procedural Order No. 8 Concerning Respondent's Request for Reconsideration of Procedural Order No. 7 (Apr. 18, 2017).

Nuclear Tests (Australia v. France), Preliminary Objections, Order, [1973] ICJ Rep. 97 (June 22, 1973).

Nuclear Tests (New Zealand v. France), [1973] ICJ Rep. 135 (June 22, 1975).

Occidental Petroleum Corporation and Occidental Exploration and Production Company v Republic of Ecuador, ICSID Case No. ARB/06/11, Decision on Provisional Measures (Aug. 17, 2007).

OOO Manolium-Processing v. Belarus, UNCITRAL, Decision on Claimant's Interim Measures Request (Dec. 1, 2018).

Perenco Ecuador Ltd. v. Republic of Ecuador and Empresa Estatal Petróleos del Ecuador (Petroecuador), ICSID Case No. ARB/08/6, Decision on Provisional Measures (May 8, 2009).

Plama Consortium Limited v. Republic of Bulgaria, ICSID Case No. ARB/03/24, Order (Sept. 6, 2005).

PNG Sustainable Development Program Ltd. V. Independent State of Papua New Guinea, ICSID Case No. ARB/13/33 (Jan. 21, 2015).

Questions relating to the Seizure and Detention of Certain Documents and Data (Timor-Leste v Australia), [2014].

Quiborax S.A., Non Metallic Minerals S.A. and Allan Fosk Kaplún v. Plurinational State of Bolivia, ICSID Case No. ARB/06/2, Decision on Jurisdiction (Sept. 27, 2002).

Quiborax S.A., Non Metallic Minerals S.A. and Allan Fosk Kaplún v. Plurinational State of Bolivia, ICSID Case No. ARB/06/2, Decision on Provisional Measures (Feb. 26, 2010).

Quiborax S.A., Non Metallic Minerals S.A. and Allan Fosk Kaplún v. Plurinational State of Bolivia, ICSID Case No. ARB/06/2, Award (Sept. 16, 2015).

Rosenne, S. THE LAW AND PRACTICE OF THE INTERNATIONAL COURT (1st edn, Leyden 1965).

RSM Production Corporation v. Santa Lucia, ICSID Case No. ARB/12/10, Decision on Saint Lucia's Request for Suspension or Discontinuation of Proceedings, ICSID Case No. ARB/12/10 (Apr. 8, 2015).

Schreuer, C. THE ICSID CONVENTION: A COMMENTARY: A COMMENTARY ON THE CONVENTION ON THE SETTLEMENT OF INVESTMENT DISPUTES BETWEEN STATES AND NATIONALS OF OTHER STATES (2009).

Seattle Totems Hockey Club v. Nat'l Hockey League, 652 F.2d 852, 855–56 (9th Cir. 1981).

Sergei Paushok and others v. Government of Mongolia, UNCITRAL, Order on Interim Measures (Sept. 2, 2008).

Sergei Viktorovich Pugachev v. Russia, UNCITRAL, Interim Award (July 7, 2007).

SGS Société Générale de Surveilance v. Pakistan, ICSID Case No. ARB/01/13, Procedural Order No. 2 (Oct. 16, 2002).

Teinver S.A., Transportes de Cercanías S.A. and Autobuses Urbanos del Sur S.A. v. Argentine Republic, ICSID Case No. ARB/09/1, Decision on Provisional Measures, (Apr. 8, 2016).

The Electricity Company of Sofia and Bulgaria (Belgium v. Bulgaria), 1939 P.C.I.J. (ser. A/B) No. 77 (Apr. 4, 1939).

Tokios Tokelés v. Ukraine, ICSID Case No. ARB/02/18, Procedural Order No. 1 (July 1, 2003).

Tokios Tokelés v. Ukraine, ICSID Case No. ARB/02/18, Procedural Order No. 3 (Jan. 18, 2005).

United Nations, STATUTE OF THE INTERNATIONAL COURT OF JUSTICE (April 18, 1946).

United Nations, VIENNA CONVENTION ON THE LAW OF TREATIES, United Nations, Treaty Series, vol. 1155 (May 23, 1969).

Víctor Pey Casado & Fondation Président Allende v. Republic of Chile, ICSID Case No. ICSID/ARB/98/2, Décision sur les Mesures Conservatoires sollicités par les Parties (Sept. 25, 2001).

www.ingramcontent.com/pod-product-compliance
Lightning Source LLC
Chambersburg PA
CBHW031334230926
51848CB00001B/227
9789004469303